QAWWAMOON

'PROTECTORS AND MAINTAINERS'

RAHMANARA CHOWDHURY

TA-HA Publishers Ltd

Ta-Ha Publishers Ltd.
© Rahmanara Chowdhury 1437 AH/ 2016 CE

First Published in September 2016
by:
Ta-Ha Publishers Ltd,
Unit 4, The Windsor Centre,
Windsor Grove, West Norwood,
London, SE27 9NT
United Kingdom
Website: www.tahapublishers.com

Written by: Rahmanara Chowdhury
General Editor: Dr. Abia Afsar-Siddiqui
Cover and Book Design: Shakir Abdulcadir > opensquares.uk

A catalogue record of this book is available from the British Library
ISBN: 978 1 84200 162 2

Printed and bound by: IMAK Ofset, Turkey

ٱلرِّجَالُ قَوَّٰمُونَ عَلَى ٱلنِّسَآءِ

"Men are the Qawwamoon
[Protectors and Maintainers] of women…"
[Qur'an 4:34]

CONTENTS

In the Name of Allah, Most Gracious, Most Merciful

INTRODUCTION

Domestic Abuse is sadly turning into an epidemic of global proportions, albeit it is very well hidden in some places. It is an area we need to understand for the sake of humanity at large and for the core of that humanity – the family unit.

Globally, one in three women will experience violence at the hands of a male partner[1], while in England and Wales, two women are killed each week by their partner or ex-partner.[2]

This book has essentially been written to bring to life in a simple and clear way, the darkness of domestic abuse and the effects it has, predominantly on victims, so that the issue can be better understood and dealt with. The approach here is specific to issues in this area within the Muslim community though domestic abuse is common to all communities, regardless of faith. It is hoped that this book will assist in instilling that sense of individual and collective responsibility we all have in dealing with this oppression that is on our very doorsteps.

It is also aimed to raise awareness within the male population of their role as 'Qawwamoon' – protectors and maintainers of women; how this responsibility and mind frame is slowly but surely disappearing

---

1   State of the World's Fathers Report, MenCare, 2015
2   Office of National Statistics, 2015

with time and hence the need to revive it. Although it is not possible to go into extensive detail as each situation needs to be dealt with on an individual basis, I have attempted to cover the most common ground and problem areas that need overcoming within different sections of the community, as per the testimonials of women who have come out of abusive marriages.

Many victims of domestic abuse find themselves without a voice after they have come out of the abuse, with very few people understanding what they have been through and how to help them. They themselves may also struggle to understand the emotions they are feeling. This book aims to give a voice to all those women who have been through domestic abuse, to bring some light into their lives, give them some hope for their future, and to show that they are entitled to feel the emotions they feel having experienced domestic abuse. It is also to show the world their hidden strength and accomplishment for having survived oppression.

Finally, this book is dedicated to the increasing number of people who have experienced being wronged and oppressed by others in their life and have struggled to come to terms with it. I hope the final section, 'On the Road to Recovery', may be of some benefit insha'Allah to all those seeking to find a way through.

My deepest thanks go to all the brave women who contributed to this writing whether directly or indirectly.

"Verily, mankind is in loss, except those who believe, and do righteous good deeds and recommend one another to the truth and recommend one another to patience."
[Qur'an: Surah 103]

QAWWAAMOON

When I was young and vulnerable
I depended on you totally
I needed you to ensure my four walls
Were those of protection, love and nurturing.
As I was meant to grow into an independent child
Able to explore the world with my little feet
I relied on you to make it an adventure
An exciting journey of development and growth.
It was the years where I was meant to be
Your little princess, safe always
One where you would mourn the thought
Of your little baby growing up and getting married one day
A day you would have to let go.
"I have no voice daddy but I need you
My very survival depends on you."

In the years of discipline and learning
My dependence on you was meant to increase but be different
The world was clear to your mature eyes
You were suppose to guide me and teach me
Direct me to that which is best for me in every way
The rules may have been strict but like a bitter medicine
You were supposed to know what would help, protect and nurture.
"I'm so young daddy, full of life and bubbling with energy
Help me to grow, be happy and maintain these qualities always."

As I developed into my young adult years
There should have been much to be celebrated
Achievements, experiences, choices and goals
They should have been mutual experiences

Times for sharing, laughter and discussions
Times for you and I both to be proud.
They should have been the baby steps
Of leaps into adulthood
You should have been there, a soft smile on your graceful face
As you pictured your little princess
And the path you had shared until now
Clinging on, yearning for a few more years
But knowing you would have to let go.
"Guide me and help me to choose with care daddy
For my heart is innocent and knows nothing else."

I entered your life as a gift from our Lord
Precious, to be looked after, protected and respected
A trust beyond trust
A sacred bond, based on affection and mercy
A chance to taste that tranquillity
In the harshness of the bitter world
Someone to lean on and be leaned on in return
Someone to give to and gain from with no expectations
A development of patience
A show of true strength was required of you.
A sign of your manhood
In the gentleness of your character,
Actions and words
A tenderness to be reciprocated
A source of strength, solace and wisdom
For mutual benefit, friendship and companionship.
"Honour me as God expects of you my companion
It's daunting and I'm trusting you."

A time of immense bonding, of exclaiming our Lord's bounty
With the welcome of little toes and fingers
Clasping trustingly at our giant sized thumbs

A chance to nurse and be the hero
A chance to let down your guards
And thrive on being you
To gain love in its full capacity
A family of your own.
Proud but not arrogant
Responsibility and duty
Not without equal respect, joy and laughter
Your supportive arms embracing me
Were meant to pave the way
For our tiny little feet
To curl up in the warmth of my lap
And from there to take its foundations
For a healthy and vibrant future.
"We are vulnerable and at your mercy, my dear
Compassion and care is what we need most."

As I grow old, the years etched into my skin
All alone now, your little feet have grown
Into strong and solid imprints
I depend on you now
Your warmth, affection and tenderness
Keeps my heart alive.
Knowing my work is almost done
But needing some last bits of companionship
To reminisce upon the days of old
To share the twinkle in my eye with.
Not much else do I ask for
Not wishing to be a burden
Content to be returning to my Lord.
"Don't let me lose my dignity
As I kept yours in your own weakness,
Embrace me with gentleness my child
Keep me nestled against your heart
As I did you."

Nikah

"And among His Signs is this, that
He created for you wives from among
yourselves, that you may find tranquillity
in them, and He has put between you
affection and mercy. Verily, in that are
indeed signs for a people who reflect."
[Qur'an 30:21]

Chapter 1

𝒩ikah: EVERY HUMAN DREAM

Marriage is something that has been around since the very creation of man himself and it is something that will remain in existence until into the hereafter. It is the human goal that most aim for, wanting one day to settle down, have a companion in life, someone to share ourselves with completely and have a deep connection with, someone to build a family and a future with. That future transcends beyond our world here on earth, into the life of the hereafter, the life yet to come. Yet as time passes by the number of divorces only increases, relationships outside of marriage only increase, single parents are on the increase. Where have we gone wrong?

There are many answers to this question but one key aspect will be brought to light here; the issue of whether we have understood what the purpose of marriage actually is. In order to understand what the purpose of marriage is we have to take a step back and examine what our purpose in life is. We all know the answer and roll it off our tongues with ease and familiarity yet how many of us have actually felt this purpose? Which of us have tasted this purpose with our very souls? How many of us have had this purpose resonate through our hearts when no one else has been around to witness this? Furthermore, how many of us have continued to carry this feeling as our very presence in our every action, word and thought? We live and exist for Allah ﷻ, to have obedience to Him and His laws in our every action, to have Him as the centre of our life and to have all things revolve around Him. That is our purpose. Yet many of us have made other things our purpose in life whether or not we realise it and marriage is one of those things. Everyone wants to get married and of course there is nothing wrong with that, for that is how we were created, with those human needs of companionship. What is wrong is when marriage becomes the only goal and focus in our life, the only thing we talk about, think about and dream of. That is not what Allah ﷻ created us for. It is a basic human need but not the purpose of our life.

There is something else we must also understand about our purpose in life. Having Allah ﷻ as the centre of our life is not because He needs that of us, indeed He transcends all needs and wants. It is us humans who require, need and rely on Allah ﷻ. Without Him, without submitting ourselves to His law, without His Wisdom and Mercy, we would be empty, desolate and barren deep within. We would be hollow human shells. A place where there is no light will be dark and full of despair. We need Him and we need to worship Him for our own sakes. No one else loses out if we do not choose this option; the only person that loses out is us as an individual.

So what happens when we get married and have had marriage as our primary focus? We may have expectations from the other person, wishing them to be a certain way, to have certain manners, to do specific things for us and take on different roles in different contexts. We go into marriage with pre-formulated ideas of what it will be like and what the other person should be like. We carry all this baggage with us into our marriage. The reality is that we should be walking into marriage without any baggage and with a clean slate, nothing written on it except the one thing we are working towards. That one thing is obedience to Allah ﷻ in our every action and deed.

Of course everything is not that black and white, for there are many differences between individuals, times, places and circumstances to consider. However, the core of our attitude should be one that we leave all of our ideas and ideals behind and focus on where we are heading with that person who will now walk that path with us. They may not take every step we do as they are equally treading their own path, but they are beside us in our journey and will shape the path we do take.

When our goal becomes Allah ﷻ, everything else will fall into place and resolving conflicts becomes easier. We know that the path will not be easy and that there will be difficulties and trials and tests along the way. If we want to succeed in those we need to understand and put into practice that it is our hereafter and our closeness to Allah ﷻ that is at stake.

The *nikah* contract itself is precisely that: a contract undertaken between the two spouses and Allah ﷻ, recognising that each will honour the other and look after the other, and it is by the words of Allah ﷻ that they are joined in marriage and are commanded to uphold their mutual responsibilities. When a person realises that Allah ﷻ is Whom they have taken that sacred contract with, then it should dawn upon them that this is no ordinary contract and therefore every effort needs to be exerted in order to ensure that all its conditions are fulfilled. The actual words of the *nikah* sermon itself should be a reminder to every man of the heavy responsibility on his shoulders of ensuring he looks after that individual who is now under his care, but few of us understand these very words let alone think about their meaning and implementation.

Chapter 2

THE PURPOSE OF
MARRIAGE

There are many purposes to marriage. One purpose of marriage touches
on the elements of mercy and compassion, for the purpose of finding
some tranquillity in the chaos of the world³, to fulfil that human need
for companionship and on a practical level, procreation. We can make
things easy for each other rather than difficult and we each have a
choice in that. It is common that we are so busy thinking of our own
needs and wants that we forget about the needs and wants of our
spouse. Yet in order to get the balance, the simple solution is for each
person to put their spouse before their own self for the sake of Allah
ﷻ and because they desire their spouse to have eternal success. When
each partner does that, a balance is created. It is when this is not upheld
by both parties that imbalances occur and things start to go wrong. We
do not need to focus on fulfilling the material wants of the here and
now except for the basic needs, yet so many of us do just that and it may
be at the expense of everlasting success as well as creating misery and
difficulty in the present life, both for ourselves and our spouse.

---

3 Qur'an 30:21

The Qur'an states:

> **"And among His Signs is this, that He created for you wives from among yourselves, that you may find tranquillity in them, and He has put between you affection and mercy. Verily, in that are indeed signs for a people who reflect."**
> [Qur'an 30:21]

Two qualities are mentioned in this verse regarding finding that tranquillity and what Allah ﷻ has placed between the hearts of the spouses. These are affection and mercy. We should take some time to really think about this and what the implications are.

Without affection a marriage becomes void of life and soul, it will wither away and die. Both spouses need affection. It does not matter that each has their flaws, for that is the nature of human beings; we have our flaws and weaknesses but we also have our positives and strengths. This is what we should be focussing on and bringing to light and reminding each other of. It is what adds softness and warmth and safety to the marriage.

The second quality is mercy. Without this mercy there is only darkness, anxiety, pain and suffering. We all make mistakes and we depend on the mercy of each other in order to overcome the mistakes we will inevitably make. If we require this for our own selves, should we not at the very least offer it in return to our spouses of all people? The closest member of our family? If we show no mercy to those whom we have greatest responsibilities towards, how can we expect to receive it in return? When we do not show mercy we only show how hard-hearted we have become and how selfish and cruel we can be. It is a reflection of how much improvement we need to make within ourselves. However, it does not have to be that way. We have a choice. With that affection and mercy, we can and should encourage each other to constantly improve for one goal only: for the pleasure of our Lord. It is a way to get closer to our Creator essentially for our own eternal success. It should be noted that encouragement is different to putting someone down and belittling others. Striving to understand the difference between the two and acting upon being encouraging will only bring us benefit and help to unite individuals.

Everyone knows that marriage is not easy and takes a lifetime of hard work and effort. That is, everyone who is married knows that and those young ones who have not had exposure to married life continue to look upon it as a bed of roses from which they assume the thorns have been removed. The reality, however, is that it is in our hands to make it easier upon each other. It is also an opportunity for each individual to truly excel in their character and raise their status with Allah ﷻ for it is within the home environment where if one can perfect their character, to no outside witnesses and for no ulterior motives except the pleasure of their Lord, that a person can truly reach a status that we cannot even begin to imagine. A person who maintains the best of character with the closest members of their family where it is normally so easy to let our standards slip and allow our emotions to get the better of us, is one who is an example to us all.

We have seen this perfect example in the life of the final Prophet ﷺ and that is what we should all be striving towards whether we are male or female, young or old. It is this very character within the privacy of our homes that prove those who have the most perfect of faith, for it is they who have that fear and consciousness of Allah ﷻ behind closed doors who understand and know that Allah ﷻ watches them though the gazes of people may not, and that it is Allah ﷻ to Whom they shall return and be accountable for their deeds to. This is a person who has perfected their faith as much as we humans are able to.

In the Qur'an we are told about spouses that "they are your garments and you are their garments".[4] What does that mean? When we look at the purpose of clothes, they are numerous: to protect us from the conditions of the weather, to protect our modesty and shame, to conceal our bodies and private aspects, to keep us warm and cool, and many more. So does this not tell us clearly what the purpose of marriage is? How we are required to be there to protect each other and maintain one another's honour and dignity? To hide from the rest of

---

4 Qur'an 2:187

the world the faults we may have and cover them up yet assist privately in self improvement? To grant each other a place of refuge and safety, shelter and protection whether physically, emotionally, psychologically or in terms of faith itself? To help beautify each other in our character, manners and conduct? Have we taken heed of these responsibilities and gifts that we can and should give to our spouse? These are questions we each need to ask ourselves and act upon. We and our spouses are the first ones that will benefit from making such changes for the sake of the One under Whose Name we have taken that sacred contract. The benefit will then automatically ripple out to all of society.

Chapter 3

MALE AND FEMALE: BACK TO BASICS

How odd it is that humans spend so much time thinking of marriage yet so little time actually preparing for it. Which of us takes the time to learn about the other gender? We may attend every marriage course that runs in the years leading up to our marriage yet what have we really gained from them? Many of us might be able to dictate the rights of the spouses yet when actually married how many concentrate on the rights of the other as opposed to always demanding their own rights? A healthy marriage is not one wherein both or one spouse is constantly reminding the other of their rights. Flexibility and putting the other first needs to be adopted in order for the affection and mercy to grow, and for the marriage to be nurtured and developed into a deep connection that lasts the tests of time and the trials of the world which cannot be avoided.

There are some things that will remain the same no matter what point in time it is, whether moments preceding the Day of Judgement, or hundreds of years before the Day of Judgement. This is why the final message of Islam is just that: the Final Message for all people, until the end of time. There are no further additions to be made and no further Prophets and Messengers to be sent. The message is complete and will always be relevant now for all people, of all times and all backgrounds.

What does this have to do with the male and the female? It is quite simple. It shows that the core nature of the male and female consists of certain traits and characteristics that will remain constant across all cross sections of the world. Obviously there will also be additional differences from influences within the environment, culture and so on, but the core is something that Allah ﷻ created and made distinct for each gender. Therefore it makes sense that we should learn about this before we actually marry the opposite gender!

We should all know that men are generally more irritable when they haven't eaten and that when they do not wish to talk about something, it means just that, hence we should give them the space to retreat and come to the conclusions they need to come to without badgering them to talk about the issue until we are blue in the face. Did the Prophet ﷺ not retreat to the cave of Hira for contemplation? Did Khadijah ؓ insist on knowing his every thought or did she give him space when he wanted it and support when he needed it?

We should all also know that women can sometimes be highly emotional and at other times cry for no apparent reason and that when they have something bothering them they need to talk about it, not necessarily seeking that anything be done, but just that they are listened to. Did Aishah ؓ not narrate how the Prophet ﷺ would check to see if she was awake at night and engage in conversation with her if she was, but let her rest if she was asleep?[5] These simple facts about the nature of the two genders alone can eliminate years of unnecessary grief yet how many people know, understand and accommodate these different natures?

The two biggest mistakes spouses make in marriages are that we try and deal with our spouse in the way that we would want to be dealt with or we approach them in the same manner that we would approach different family members of that gender, for example our mum or sister or brother. Your spouse is not you and nor are they a blood relative of yours, therefore the same rules do not apply and should not be applied. By default we cannot expect that our spouse will

---

5　Sahih Bukhari, hadith number 258

deal with situations in exactly the same way that we would and nor can we expect that just because our sister or brother reacts in a certain way, our wife or husband will do the same. Our relationships with the opposite gender in a bloodline family context will be completely different to our relationship within marriage. This is one of the factors which makes marriage unique in itself.

In his book, 'Men are from Mars and Women are from Venus', John Gray identifies the emotional needs of men and women. It is simple and straightforward in outlining the different natures of men and women yet many of us scorn at seeking such knowledge, usually to our own detriment. These needs can be summarised as follows:[6]

'PRIMARY 'EMOTIONAL 'NEEDS OF 'WOMEN

Compassion – Having that concern and showing that you care and are mindful of the needs of your wife, even if you cannot always meet them.

Understanding – Allowing her to speak her mind without passing judgements, but with an openness and closeness that allows her to come to you anytime anything is on her mind, shows that she is understood by you. You don't need to have any answers for her but just offer her the comfort of having you to turn to without being rejected.

Respect – Knowing that you will respect her and ensure her honour is never compromised and that she can rely on you to protect her, will make your wife feel honoured and proud to be your wife. It will raise your status in her eyes. She will know that you are truly her garment, there to fulfil your responsibilities towards her. Honouring her both in public and private will reinforce this and strengthen your bond; only honouring her with such respect in one of these contexts will cause her to distance herself from you and not trust you.

---

6 The headings under the 'Primary Emotional Needs of Women' and 'Primary Emotional Needs of Men' have been taken from Gray, 2005. Explanations are the author's own. For further information about the topic, see Yasir Qadhi, 2013.

Validation – When your wife takes the courage to speak up about her emotions and things that have been on her mind, or just in general, men can easily fall into the trap of invalidating how she feels without meaning to. Examples include by telling her she is being silly or by trying to explain away what she is saying. This can leave a woman feeling totally unheard and unloved. Regardless of whether the issue is something major or not, just accepting that your wife has certain emotions about it will validate what she feels and therefore she will feel that it is safe to be open with you in the future and that you will understand and not make her feel insignificant or worthless.

Devotion – When your wife feels that you have special deep feelings for her, she will feel loved and very special and no one will be able to take your place. She will hold these emotions close to her heart and she will hold you deep within her heart. You will have secured her loyalty and devotion in return. The simple act of ensuring you give your wife a regular hug, or make daily physical non intimate contact, for example, just by sitting next to her or stroking her face or touching her arm will reinforce this message.

Reassurance – Women need regular reassurance of your emotional connection and of your love. You will not lose anything by often telling your wife that you love her – you will only gain her admiration, love and loyalty in return. Men can often expect that their wife should know he loves her, but letting her know regularly and reinforcing it with positive and caring action does not cost anything and will only strengthen the affection and bond between you and will bring much comfort to your wife, beyond what you can imagine.

PRIMARY EMOTIONAL NEEDS OF MEN

Trust – A man needs to know that his wife has complete and total trust in him to do the best of his ability always and that even if things do not go as planned, you will not be there to point the finger at him but rather be there to assure him that you knew he did his best. Without this he will be left feeling inadequate and undermined, which will cause friction and distance to develop.

Encouragement – Giving that positive encouragement and support will provide your husband with the drive and motivation he needs to not just achieve, but to excel in whatever he undertakes. By being encouraging as opposed to pointing out failings and errors, you will sow the seeds of support and will give the message to your husband that he has a solid foundation that he can always turn to and lean on for support.

Approval – Undermining your husband and the reasons behind his actions are another easy trap that many can fall into. This shows disapproval towards him and his thinking without any room for making mistakes. When you show your husband that you approve of his leadership skills and decision making, it will strengthen him and help him keep that focus on developing qualities that are already instilled within him but may just need nurturing, growth and experience.

Appreciation – When you appreciate your husband and all that he does for you, it will motivate him to do more for you and ensure your needs are being put first. It is such a simple concept that many fail to realise or adopt. Instead our minds are easily dominated by expectations and demands rather than focussing on appreciating all that we get from our spouses. This means that where we can actually be receiving emotional support and uplift one another, we instead inflict darkness and drag each other down.

Acceptance – None of us are perfect and hence we should not expect that our spouse will be perfect either. When you show unreserved acceptance to your husband of all his qualities, both strengths and weaknesses, it will show him that he does not need to hide any part of himself from you and that he can be himself around you. In return he will naturally accept you and all your strengths, weaknesses and moods. By not accepting him and constantly pointing out the things he needs to change, you will have the opposite effect to what you wanted and make him feel inadequate and unmotivated to make any positive changes for the benefit of the marriage.

Admiration – By showing your husband how much you admire him and all the unique traits he has as well as the unique qualities of your relationship, you are providing him with a stable and solid platform from which he will only strive to be better to you as a husband. This will send him the clear message that you love and admire him and have noticed what is special about him, giving him a lightness that he can carry around with him wherever he may be and cause him to smile inwardly when thinking about you.

It cannot be said that these different needs are totally exclusive to each gender, as naturally we can see that there will be some overlap. However, the key thing to note is that these are the primary needs of each gender based upon their natural make up and therefore can be used as a general guideline for mutual benefit.

Chapter 4

GENDER ROLES WITHIN MARRIAGE

In the past it was easier to identify the roles of each gender and thus meet each other's needs with much better outcomes. However, with the demands of everyday living and often human imposed thoughts and ideologies of how we should be living, this has changed and meant that the lines of our individual roles have become blurred within marriage. This naturally tips the requirement of each spouse in terms of emotional needs and means both spouses need to invest more effort in appreciating and supporting one other.

There is no fixed rule for all, every marriage is different with different individuals and dynamics to consider. It is allowing this very flexibility that will help in ensuring marriages go from strength to strength. In marriages where both spouses are able to establish together what their roles are, it will contribute to helping them set strong and stable foundations from which they can then build upon. However, when the marriage is based on blurred roles, this is when problems start to creep in and slowly over time exacerbate, eventually even leading to marital breakdown. The confusion that can come about from this blurring of roles will often be difficult for most individuals to re-organise in their minds let alone on a practical level.

The starting point to clarifying gender roles is that both spouses must individually and then together go back to what their own purpose in life is and what each thinks the purpose of their marriage is. It may seem odd to commence from each person assessing their individual purpose in life and marriage when we generally know what our purpose in life is. We do, of course, have an umbrella expression helping to give our life direction, however, within this there is room for individuals to exercise their individuality and still be fulfilling their main purpose in life. Therefore, it is only healthy for all relationships to recognise that each spouse is an individual who has a personal take on how they wish to fulfil their life goals and then work to merge that positively with a collective family goal within their marriage. Furthermore, each spouse needs to take responsibility for themselves as individuals because they are accountable to Allah ﷻ for their deeds regardless of whether their spouse is present or absent. When that is done then it becomes easier to identify what our roles are within marriage, how to establish that balance and obtain that fulfilment in marriage, life and goals for the hereafter. It must be done together so that both spouses know where they stand with each other and are of a common understanding, working towards their goals from the same platform.

The second step is then for the couple to discuss and reach mutual agreement upon how their different objectives and roles fit within different elements of their shared life. For example, what will be each person's role with regards to earning, doing the household chores, raising children, relations with extended family, community involvement, seeking knowledge, collective health and fitness and so forth. Each couple can decide for themselves what the most appropriate categories are and move forward from there. It is also a good idea to regularly review these roles in order to ensure you both are on the same page as well as to introduce some healthy changes to the relationship.

Chapter 5

ASPIRING TOWARDS THE TRUE ISLAMIC CHARACTER

Marriage is a gift that we can often overlook until it goes wrong. When we are given something special and precious, we would naturally do our utmost to look after it and keep it protected and maintained. We would put it in a special place out of harm's way. Marriage is one of those very gifts that we need to be giving that special treatment to yet so often we fail to.

It starts with purity of intention in that we want to please our Creator in the blessing that He has bestowed upon us and part of our appreciation for this gift is that we strive and are persistent in ensuring we are doing the best that we can within our marriage. When both spouses are doing this, it can only be a positive investment into the future of that marriage. We also need to have the pure intention of wanting the best for our spouse because they are first and foremost our fellow human and Muslim, and secondly, because they are our spouse whom we should naturally want the best for, not just the bare minimum. If each spouse spent the amount of time thinking of the rights the other has upon them and catering to these rather than what they may be missing out upon, then that would be the start of a drastic pull towards ensuring the best is being sought after for this marriage.

There are so many key qualities we should aim to have in general but for marriages to survive with all the external pressures, let alone the pressures within families and couples themselves, there are a few essential qualities we need to strive to perfect or excel in. Without such qualities our marriages will become stale, dead and lifeless, a heavy burden wrapped around us, dragging us back in daily life and maybe even in our hereafter. It is so easy within the home life to let go of the best conduct which can be an eternal disaster for us, hence why it is all the more important to maintain our vigilance in our conduct and character at home, with our families.

COMPASSION AND MERCY

Without compassion and mercy there would be no hope for any of us. Which of us can claim to be perfect and flawless? Which of us can claim to have never made a mistake? Which of us can claim to have never sinned? Our knowledge of our imperfections and errors should drive us to understand that if we show no mercy to others and the mistakes they will inevitably make, how can we possibly expect to get the same in return? In some cases, how dare we expect this, in return for not giving it? That is simply outrageous.

Marriages need the ingredient of that mercy the spouses have towards each other, otherwise no marriage would ever survive. This mercy and compassion is not just any old quality either, it is absolutely crucial and essential to every single marriage regardless of time, age or culture. It is one of the very foundations of marriage. It is a quality we cannot afford to be without or neglect. Our own future depends upon it. It is not necessary to take your spouse to account for every little thing they have done and not done. We do not have the right to delve into past mistakes and private sins especially when we have married that person based upon the good qualities we and others saw in them at that time. We do not need to have unreasonable expectations of our spouse that are endless – that is the best ingredient for creating misery and unhappiness. By adopting that mercy and compassion we give ourselves permission to enjoy the good aspects of our marriage and spouse and to overlook the negative aspects that may not always be possible to change or to our ideal levels. We open up the doors of possibilities within our marriage and create lightness and warmth that we can genuinely enjoy and find some tranquillity within.

FORGIVENESS

A person who chooses not to forgive only does one thing; they destroy their own goodness and their heart will be overpowered by this sour rancour. It will weigh heavy on their backs and eventually destroy the person themselves. It will not harm the person to whom it is directed at. It serves no purpose but self destruction. Every marriage requires forgiveness. Otherwise every spouse will forever be afraid to be human when grudges are being held against them and they receive no forgiveness. Without forgiveness there is no laughter and joy, no smiling over silly mistakes, no sharing of experiences, and no personal growth and development. There is no helping and supporting each other.

Marriages also need to be based upon forgiveness for the very reason that if we cannot do without it, how can we expect our spouse to do without? If we want to keep our marriage alive then we need to give it life. Forgiveness is a breath of fresh energised life back into any situation, an opportunity to rise again, to increase our efforts, to better ourselves, to support those most closest to us, and to allow for us to stand taller in our determination. By not forgiving we slice off our own feet at the ankles therefore causing us to fall flat on our faces with little chance of standing up again. And then we wonder why things never improve.

HUMILITY

Often we do not give this characteristic much thought within the context of our marital life, but it is another key ingredient in appreciating that our spouse is a human being just like us, with strengths in some areas and limited capabilities in others. They are not perfect, they have flaws, they will make mistakes, sometimes they may need a bit of guidance and steering, sometimes they may need your strength and support. Other times it will be you needing their strength and support, their advice and guidance, their reminders about your responsibilities towards Allah ﷻ. A humble heart can admit to their faults and mistakes and take on board what others have to say without thinking we are not in need of such advice. We may have a tendency to think we always know best, but those closest to us may be able to see some things with much more clarity and vision and it would only benefit us to utilise this.

A humble heart feels shyness in their every deed that Allah ﷻ is watching them and they will be held accountable for all that they do and say. A humble heart therefore does not put their spouse in a difficult situation and impose burdens upon them concerning worldly life. Instead at the core of their every action will be the remembrance of where they have come from and where they are going. Being humble does not mean to allow others to walk all over us, that is something else altogether.

If within a marriage both spouses have understood their purpose in life and their purpose in marriage, then it leads to the natural conclusion that our spouse is there to help us and protect us and look out for us. Therefore any suggestions they may make do not need to be taken negatively or to the detriment of the marriage. A humble heart will be open to their input and work with them and even go back and check with them on their character and personal development. A humble heart will realise and understand that when you look down upon the earth from above, all humans become insignificant little dots, each running around in our own world taking on our lives as though we are important. In the greater picture of the universe we become insignificant and unimportant. Yet we can reach heights of success through our character and sincere good treatment of others. Our physical being may be insignificant but our actions, deeds, kindness, compassion and humbleness can help us to reach some success with our Creator. That is what gives us weight.

CONTINUOUS STRIVING FOR IMPROVEMENT

A marriage where there is no continuous striving for personal improvement will soon be stagnant and polluted. It will reflect the deadness within the heart. Every second that passes is more precious than any of us can even begin to imagine yet the irony is that we will only realise this when that last second on earth has passed us by. Then the regrets will overpower us.

Every marriage needs movement. If we do not strive to make this movement a positive one then guaranteed there will be other negative movements in place of this. That continuous positive shift in marriage comes from that personal growth and development humans can get through different life experiences, through learning and reflection, through human interaction. This will naturally help us to re-invest in our marriages time and again with one crucial added ingredient – if we allow it. For it may be that we can go through many different life experiences and lead every day of our lives yet we truly never learn or gain anything from either of these; our minds do not develop, our hearts do not grow, and our souls remain locked in one place. We have to start with the right attitude in wanting to improve ourselves first before any of the steps we take can actually benefit us, and therefore the steps and efforts we make to grow and develop ourselves must then be something that we continuously strive in.

It is easy in life to get comfortable in certain routines and ways of doing things that we forget that there are other alternatives and options out there which may actually be better for us. It is this heedlessness and lethargy towards ourselves and our responsibilities that is one of the root causes of problems going from bad to worse.

If we are truly sincere to Allah ﷻ, then we would always want to be striving in improving ourselves even if that means trying out new things that stretch us in different ways. Sincerity in this does not mean constantly pointing the finger at your spouse either. When you strive and make real efforts in this within your own self, it will become contagious and you will only be encouraging your spouse to do the same without any negativity. Of course it is also down to every individual to realise their own responsibilities and be sincere in that. If we are able to sit on the sidelines and watch our spouse go from strength to strength without feeling any motivation to do the same, then we have not fully understood our purpose in life. A marriage requires both spouses to strive in every area, not just one.

Chapter 6

ACHIEVING TRUE MARITAL INTIMACY

It is the one thing every couple wishes to achieve, that true marital intimacy between the spouses in order to have a long lasting and healthy relationship wherein each person can find that unshakeable support and fulfilment. Achieving that true marital intimacy starts with knowing ourselves first. If we do not know ourselves, our nature, what triggers us to behave and think in a certain way, why we do certain things and such, then how can we expect our spouse to understand us?

It is our own individual responsibility to ensure that whatever we may have experienced of life prior to getting married, we understand how these experiences have shaped us without carrying any burdens into our marriage expecting that our spouse will sort everything out for us. Even if issues have not been sorted and we have not dealt with or come to terms with certain life experiences, the main point is that we understand what these issues are and how they have shaped us and are actively doing something about problematic areas. Where our spouse-to-be has a right to know about certain things, then we should reveal these things in order that each individual can make an informed decision rather than having regrets later on.

Once we understand ourselves then it will be easier for our spouse to understand us and provide a solid foundation from which true marital intimacy can be achieved. There may be things that require support from our spouses on a long term basis, indeed every marriage has something wherein each spouse needs to support each other, but the key thing is that we take on our individual responsibilities and do not expect that our spouse will sort everything out for us and essentially 'fix us' or 'fix' themselves to suit us. They can hold our hand along the way but it is unfair to expect them to carry us permanently.

Marital intimacy cannot be achieved without both spouses putting in continuous effort. Intimacy is a two way thing and will not materialise with only one spouse working on it. Once both individuals understand this and have understood their own natures then marital intimacy can be worked upon, and it does require work and building up over time; it will not just occur overnight. A truly healthy marriage with full intimacy between the spouses will have that deep connection and understanding on every level of the marriage including psychological, emotional, physical, operational, social and spiritual. In each of these areas each spouse will be there to support the other, will understand the temperament of their spouse and their mood patterns, their needs and special areas that require extra support, will negotiate where possible in order to make things easy upon each other, will give an equal contribution, will affirm one another and will be able to enjoy one another. All of this is limited if we do not first and foremost understand ourselves.

The Human Impact of Abuse

DEDICATED TO ALL THE WOMEN WHO HAVE SHARED THE FOLLOWING...

I am angry that I was nothing more than an object to you, that you saw me and treated me as only an object.

I am angry that you arrogantly tried to play God. You twisted the beautiful way of God to satisfy your sick need to get control over me then you made out to be the hero by supposedly forgiving me!

I am angry that you absolved yourself of taking any responsibility for your actions to the extent of not even bothering to apologise towards the end, claiming to be in such a state that you could not remember the things you had said and done.

I am angry that I don't know who you really are and that you pretended to be someone you were not, yet accused me of this. If you think it was being clever then think again. It's called manipulation and deceit, something very different to clever.

I am angry that you made me feel pity for you to the extent that I gave you every penny I had. How can you live with yourself as you consume my money while I live in debt?

I am angry that you have taken away my ability to work. You have severed my lifeline.

I am angry that you put on one face to the rest of the world yet you were the extreme opposite to me. I wish you would not be so destructive.

I am angry for all the names you called me and how much you put me down and made me loathe myself, yet you claimed you could not remember.

I am angry for all the violence you inflicted on me, the one you were entrusted with, a covenant you made with God to protect and look after - how could you even raise your voice let alone your hand to a woman under your care?

I am angry that you knew of my poor health yet that did not stop your violence. When you went for me you would not stop, fists clenched, repeatedly punching in a cold calculating manner and hitting against any surface you could get access to, over and over.

I am angry that you dragged me around and then told me I was free to leave yet had locked the doors and taken my keys. What sick games you played, what did you get out of it?

I am angry that you stamped on my face; you treated me like I was sub-human.

I am angry that you could kick me over and over while I lay motionless curled up on the floor.

I am angry that you nearly dislocated my shoulder but you did not even suggest that I go to the doctors, instead I was left to suffer for weeks.

I am angry that you would not even glance at the purple and green bruises on my arms and thighs.

I am angry that the only thing I saw in your eyes after you had head-butted me in the face was the worry about how I would conceal my black eye. I thought it was remorse at the time but actually you were only worried about yourself.

I am angry that you slapped me so hard that I cannot swallow properly due to nerve damage.

I am angry that I know what it is liked to be slapped so hard that you see lights.

I am angry that you would spit in my face. Do you know how ugly you looked when doing this?

I am angry that you strangled me so many times and looked like you meant what you said, that you would enjoy watching me die. When you did this and put your face up to mine you would look like a monster, your face contorted into the face of something very very ugly.

I am angry that you expected me to be ok and normal and close to you despite whatever you did. You killed my heart a thousand times over.

I am angry that I was terrified of you and that I could tell when you would be violent, yet I could do nothing about it and had to spend time with you, only to have that utter dread and darkness hanging over me.

I am angry that you sat and ate the food that I specially bought and prepared for you, after you had severely beaten me up. You had no shame. You suffocated my world. You drained the life out of me.

I am angry that you pushed me with such force that I have never felt pain that severe travel up my spine as I fell. I wondered if I would survive. You were so heartless, you saw my pain and yet did nothing.

I am angry that I could not do more to stop you during the violence.

I am angry, very angry, that you would twist things around with such deceit that I would then take the blame and beg for your forgiveness and beg you to put up with me. And that I had to buy gifts and do things to make it up to you. Even then you would wear me down relentlessly because I was not doing enough or not being affectionate enough.

I am angry that you made daily life hell for me by watching my every move and timing my every action including going to the bathroom.

I am angry that I had to show you my phone contents regularly yet you were already spying on me and my phone unbeknownst to me.

I am angry that you would keep me awake for hours in an argument that just went round in circles over the tiniest of actions that I had failed to do in the exact manner you wished. Then of course you would blame me and make me feel guilty. You burdened me beyond anything.

I am angry that you isolated me from everyone and everything. I was no longer a person but just your shadow. I was not even allowed to think for myself despite your false claims. You squashed and trampled me as a person.

I am angry that I always had to be affectionate towards you, yet you were allowed to be in whatever mood you chose to be whenever you chose.

I am angry that you made me dependent on you, yet you were not there to meet my basic needs.

I am angry that I could not even go shopping for food without you stressing me out to such an extent that I stopped going unless I absolutely had to which meant that I was hardly eating.

I am angry that you put every aspect of me and my life under a microscope and made me feel like nothing and like there was nothing good about me or my life.

I am angry that you stole those years of my life and even now I am wasting time because of you.

I am angry that I do not know how many others have suffered in the same way at your hands.

I am angry that I did not listen to my doubts at the very start.

I am absolutely furious about the endless oaths you made me take on matters that had nothing to do with you. Did you think you were God? You caused me much darkness and anguish.

I am angry that you badgered me for months on end on things you decided to make an issue. That was just pathetic, but it was burden upon burden upon burden.

I am angry that you slandered my name. How do you think you will stand before God with such an accusation? How dare you make such a false accusation? You are a fraud through and through.

I am angry that you tried to make friends and family think that I was crazy. It just reaffirmed your true colours.

I am angry that you caused me so much daily anguish and trauma that I literally could not even think and every day became about minimal survival. I no longer cared if I lived or not.

I am angry that you felt entitled to take from me whatever you wanted yet gave nothing in return, nor acknowledged that I had any needs as a human except when you gained something.

I am angry that I had to pretend to be ok so no one would guess what you were putting me through while you were always the perfect citizen to the outside world.

I am angry that I tried to leave, but could not explain to anyone properly about why because so much of what you did was deception, manipulation and betrayal on a level beyond my comprehension.

I am angry that you do not understand the reality of life and change your ways.

Chapter 1

UNDERESTIMATING THE IMPACT

Unless one works specifically in the field or has gone through or witnessed domestic abuse, most people are very much unaware of the true extent of the human impact of abuse on an individual, any children and in effect, society at large. This can have dangerous consequences especially upon the victim and for overall society in the long term. In the worst case scenario, we have seen people take their own lives or have the perpetrator murder them after some time. In some cases it is not unknown that the victim themselves or their children may attempt to kill the perpetrator due to the severity of the impact of the abuse. When an issue is not properly understood or is underestimated, it means the root causes can never be fully tackled and therefore other social problems resulting from this will only get worse with time. Society as a whole will end up feeling the consequences of what may easily be deemed as a 'private' problem. It is not a private problem. It is a problem that we need to deal with collectively in society for the long term protection and betterment of everyone.

In order to fully understand the impact we must first look at some of what victims have experienced. Below is just a brief summary of what most women who have gone through domestic abuse would have experienced, whether that be all or some from each area, or concentrated in specific areas.

PSYCHOLOGICAL
> Degradation
> Mind games
> Lying
> Minimisation of abuse
> Outright denial of abuse
> 'Walking on eggshells' feeling
> Control of thoughts
> Twisting words and the truth

EMOTIONAL
> Being made to feel inadequate
> Mothering skills criticised
> Never good enough
> Devalued
> Name calling
> Being forced to give affection
> Getting little or no affection, care or consideration in return
> Unfaithfulness
> Being made to feel sub-human

PHYSICAL
> Broken bones
> Scarring
> Cuts and bruises
> Pushing and shoving
> Threats
> Spitting
> Pulling hair
> Punching and slapping
> Made to bleed
> Kicking
> Preventing access to medical needs
> Injuries causing long term health issues

SEXUAL
> Forcing sex
> Degrading acts
> Objectification
> Inappropriate language
> No regard for health/pregnancies
> Refusal of intimacy rights
> False accusations about chastity

FINANCIAL
> Taking money
> Not allowing access to money
> Unauthorised financial contracts
> Having to ask for money for basic needs
> Accessing spouse bank account without consent
> Depositing and withdrawing personal funds from spouse account
> Using children's money for personal spending

SPIRITUAL
> Dictating beliefs
> Preventing or limiting practice/prayer
> Demanding constant attention
> Preventing learning
> Imposing personal preferences
> Limiting sources of knowledge

These are just a minor snapshot of the domination, cruelty and subjugation a victim of domestic abuse may have been exposed to consistently over a period of time. A person who is exposed to any or all of these over any duration of time will not be left without some impact upon them. In abusive relationships, the impact is made much worse by either the fact that the duration may be a long period, or even in cases of a shorter period, the level of abuse may have been highly damaging. Domestic abuse can be said to be a systematic annihilation of an individual on every single facet of their being.

Bearing the above in mind, the impact of domestic abuse will be discussed based on these individual areas. According to each individual and each situation, the impact will differ; what may be applicable in one situation may not be in another. The discussion is not fully extensive due to the severity and vastness of the impact domestic abuse has on everyday life. Instead the most prominent issues are presented. It is hoped that by drawing attention to these effects on a human level, it will present a clearer picture for outsiders thus better equipping them to help. It is also hoped that it will bring some peace of mind to victims in validation of their different feelings and experiences and to know that they are not alone in them.

Chapter 2

PSYCHOLOGICAL IMPACT

Research conducted by Women's Aid has shown that 64% of women admitted into psychiatric care in the UK have previously suffered from domestic abuse.[7] This stark statistic alone shows how the impact of abuse can destroy lives and the long term future for such individuals, especially if they do not receive the right help and support in overcoming their experiences. Much more about the severity of this need not be said for it is self explanatory that a person's life becomes so unbearable and their psychological state becomes so unhealthy, that they are unable to function on a daily basis without severe medical intervention.

For those who try to get on with life they may face many everyday challenges, for example, constant paranoia that they are being watched. In a lot of cases this will be due to the fact that they are actually being stalked. In other cases it will be because they were stalked previously or know how controlling their spouse was and so live with the after-effect that he is not likely to just get on and leave them alone so quickly. The fear and 'on edge' state this can leave an individual in may sound minor to some, but the reality of living with having to constantly look over your shoulder out of fear is something any individual will find disabling and be the cause of much anxiety.

---

7 Women's Aid, 2011

One of the largest psychological impacts of abuse can be the total loss of self confidence and self esteem. It may sound trivial on paper but the reality for women who have had to endure this can be a living nightmare and leave them totally bereft and confused about anything and everything. Associated with this is the feeling that every action and word they utter needs to be justified in order for others to accept it, followed by the constant apologising for contributing to conversations or asking for anything, or even speaking in general. These have been survival methods required during the abuse and need to be unlearnt once out of the abusive situation. A task that is much easier said than actually done; for some women this process may take years to unlearn.

Often many victims will blame themselves and feel ashamed and embarrassed at others knowing what they have been through. Without the right help and support, they will continue to carry that self blame and guilt which would have been instilled deeply within their minds by the perpetrator. One comment from outsiders, friends or family that passes a negative judgement upon them indicating that they were at fault, can solidify in the victim's mind everything the perpetrator has tried to lead them to believe. Hence even though they may have now left the situation, that one comment can pull them back psychologically so that they are then unable to free themselves of guilt that they need not feel. When a perpetrator uses tactics to abuse and control in this systematic way, whatever the victim does is of no significance, he will take out on her whatever he wishes to in the manner he chooses regardless of what she does.

When outsiders who can potentially help then turn around and impose their own judgements and comments, whether based on culture or lack of understanding, they are in essence re-enacting forms of the abuse the victim has already undergone. Therefore to her it may feel like she has left one abusive situation only to end up under further oppression by those around her. This will only exacerbate her isolation and vulnerability and in some cases can lead to the victim going back to the perpetrator who then inflicts worse abuse on her than previously.

Many women, and indeed children, can also be left with Post Traumatic Stress Disorder (PTSD), often sadly undiagnosed by medical professionals but clearly visible to other support workers. Post Traumatic Stress is something that was originally associated with veterans of war due to what they had been exposed to while out in war. However, it now includes victims of domestic abuse who themselves have suffered trauma. From having felt that danger to their very lives and well being and being helpless in that situation, they find that they are stuck in that trauma, unable to shift the emotions they are feeling and thus exhibit the same PTSD symptoms, remaining in a state of psychological shock. PTSD can occur in three main areas: actually re-experiencing the trauma, avoiding reminders of the traumas to severe degrees and having significantly increased levels of anxiety and emotional states.

The manifestations can range from flashbacks, nightmares, recurrent memories, difficulty sleeping, physiological reactions such as increased heart rate and panic attack symptoms, intense distress, significant loss of interest in general life, detachment from others, sense of having a very limited future, going to lengths to avoid any reminder of the trauma such as places, smells, food etc., frequent hyper vigilant state of alert, difficulties concentrating and outbursts of different strong emotions. These are but to just name a few of the consequences that can be absolutely disabling for normal everyday living - something which victims often find difficult to understand themselves let alone then have to explain to others.

Chapter 3

EMOTIONAL IMPACT

In one way, shape or form, a victim will have been degraded and put down and made to feel worthless. She may have heard this time and again and had it emphasised and demonstrated to her in many different ways. Once a person hears something more than a couple of times it becomes reinforced in their minds, hence having this self belief, value and worth is something that all victims will need a lot of support with in overcoming. It will be some time before they can start to think they have value again let alone fully believe it and start to live that out in their daily life. This will naturally have a knock-on effect on their confidence and thus their ability to do normal things and to have normal conversations with people. They may be constantly doubting themselves or thinking they are not good enough or should not be having their own views and opinions on subjects as that is what they were led to believe about themselves.

Holding down a job, or even getting one in the first place, will seem like a mountain to a victim who has had every ounce of self confidence squeezed out of her. Being a confident mother and making decisions and sticking by them may seem alien to her, with constant self criticism and having had her ability to do what she is naturally able to taken away from her. Being in public places or around lots of people may cause high levels of anxiety or bring on a panic attack because she is remembering his words in her head or she no longer knows how to cope in such settings due to having been isolated from everyone for so long. The people around her will be expecting her to be normal again now that she is away from the perpetrator but they have not looked to see the wounds that are not visible to the naked eye and the damage that has been left behind but not yet treated.

As for moving onto a new relationship or even building new and old friendships, there will be the natural consequences of trusting another person to that extent ever again. Having this trust destroyed is something that will take time to rebuild with every person in her life. People would have judged her both whilst she was in that abusive situation and once she is out of it and this will have only have added to her guards being put up more than most people. There is no doubt she will be in a state of emotional isolation, with very few people, if any, understanding what she is feeling and why.

She may go the opposite way and no longer understand what healthy boundaries are due to having all natural and normal healthy boundaries broken at every turn. This may therefore lead her to break down in front of every person she meets with a need to tell them her story and personal experiences as well as latching onto people easily. This obviously can lead to her being taken advantage of further or by preying individuals, or cause further anguish by people who simply are insensitive or lack empathy and understanding.

Where others may know her to be a very able and capable individual with a lot to offer, she herself may be experiencing a lot of internal self criticism that stops her being active and outgoing in normal things, and thereby hindering her achieving her full potential or just living a normal daily life.

Chapter 4

PHYSICAL IMPACT

The most obvious of the physical effects of abuse are those which leave a direct visible sign on the body as a result of one-off or repeated assaults. The range of such injuries is wide and varied. However, in addition to this, many victims are also left with further long or short term physical consequences of all that they have been through.

They may find it many months if not years before they are able to have proper healthy sleeping patterns without medical assistance. They may develop eating disorders and exhibit symptoms of intense stress and anxiety due to having a heightened state of awareness to danger, even when there may be no danger present. There will be the consequences of unexplained illnesses due to all the stress their body has been through or being increasingly prone to pick up bugs and infections and other illnesses due to their immune system being so run down.

Memories and trigger factors including times, dates, places, foods, smells and the like may spark off panic attacks or provoke intense anxiety for someone who has not had professional help in overcoming these. The results of the impact in the other areas discussed will also start showing on the individual in different ways whether by weight increase or loss, hair loss or white hair, totally isolating oneself or not being able to stay alone, recurrent exhaustion, and avoiding physical contact with anyone to but name a few. There may also be attempts at self harm or suicide.

Unless these issues are dealt with and victims receive the proper help and support they require, the chances of developing ongoing medical conditions will naturally be more likely. The human body, as amazing as it is, can only be put through so much before it becomes overburdened and run down.

Chapter 5

SEXUAL
IMPACT

Sexual intimacy between spouses is something that is healthy and encouraged. In an abusive relationship, the healthy aspect to this is taken away and left with raw unhealthy patterns of behaviour that many victims find naturally totally degrading but are unable to speak about. Healthy boundaries and expectations are ripped away and replaced with derogatory behaviour, expectations and demands whether spoken or unspoken.

For a victim to learn what is healthy and not, means going into some of the most personal aspects of her relationship with her spouse which would naturally be difficult for any person. This is often coupled with the guilt that others may place on her that she should not speak about such things, because of the false belief that the religion or cultural norms do not permit it. That is not to say that she is advertising every aspect of her marriage, but just that it is permitted to seek professional confidential help and advice due to having gone through a major trauma and needing help for her personal recovery.

For moving on in her life eventually and remarrying, there may be many fears which could be dealt with prior to her entering that relationship, through that professional help and encouragement from friends and family. Victims may at the extreme end decide to never re-marry, instead hating all men. Others may end up having numerous unhealthy relationships as a release for the self-loathing they feel or because they have not been taught how to spot the warning signs of abusive relationships and perpetrators, and sadly because they have not been valued by others so they feel they deserve such treatment.

For those who are able to move forward in their life and rebuild a positive future for themselves, they may have the fear of being anywhere near a male or anxiety related to male presence. It may be that actual intimacy requires a lot of time and patience or that they carry forward unhealthy patterns which they think are the norm due to their past experience. In some cases, the victim will have been led to believe that her sexual needs are shameful and unimportant and that she should have no needs where as the *deen* clearly demonstrates the total opposite, in that ensuring the needs of the wife are stressed before the husband meets his own needs. Shame is imposed upon her to refrain from seeking the help she may need to build a new healthy family, where as in the *deen* there is no shame in asking for gaining knowledge for the betterment of oneself and society. These are facts that will be alien to most victims of domestic abuse, especially those who have suffered sexual abuse in particular.

Understanding healthy boundaries within healthy relationships will also be unfamiliar territory, for the rules that are put in place in abusive relationships are completely the opposite to what a healthy relationship consists of. What is healthy conduct and what is not as well as rulings regarding permissibility and impermissibility will all need to be revisited in order to check proper understanding and so that destructive behaviours are not carried forward where they need not be.

In essence there are a lot of broken pieces in every aspect of a victim's life that she slowly needs to pick up and put back together. The more help and understanding she has, the more chances she has of achieving that outcome. The less help and understanding she has, the less likely she is of ever having any goals to aspire towards in the first place.

Chapter 6

FINANCIAL IMPACT

In most situations of domestic abuse, the perpetrator will normally control the finances, including any income relating to the victim, in line with his control and domination of every other aspect of their relationship. A woman leaving this situation will commonly not have any money at all. If she has some, then it may be that she has to now learn how to manage finances in a healthy way. If she was one of the rare victims allowed to control her own finances, again she still may need to learn how to manage this in a healthy way due to having had to manage it within unhealthy boundaries previously.

Some perpetrators will not want to lose control of the financial 'privileges' they experienced whilst being with the victim whether this ranges from access to any assets she may have had or income relating to any children they have. Therefore they may go as far as fighting for child custody purely for monetary gain, as well as being a form of continuing their abusive control tactics despite the victim having left them. Others will refuse to pay child maintenance leaving victims who are often unable to go out to work, in extremely difficult financial circumstances, usually with debts piling high under their name but having been initiated by the perpetrator.

The financial control is one aspect of both the effects and the after-effects of domestic abuse that many outsiders remain oblivious to. What they are instead exposed to is normally the perpetrator, who is granted access to the children, showering them with expensive gifts, toys and gadgets. Few pick up on the fact that these are continued tactics the perpetrator is playing out, as that is all he is able to do now without anyone pointing accusatory fingers at him. With regards to actually feeding and clothing any children and looking after their true daily needs and ongoing growth and development, this is something that often gets overlooked by onlookers.

Many victims of domestic abuse have felt the impact of this as far as within court proceedings and verdicts regarding child custody, because the perpetrator has been able to show much more financial stability than she has. Women have and do lose their children to perpetrators due to this. The long term consequence on the mother who loses her children in such a way does not need explanation. Neither do the long term consequences for a society where children are being raised according to tactics and manipulation, rather than with love and encouragement for growth and development.

Chapter 7

SPIRITUAL
IMPACT

Anyone who has come to the *deen* after not having had it in their lives knows the true value of the gift that they have been blessed with. Even for those who have had it but have felt an increase in their spiritual understanding and development over time, it is simply priceless. A perpetrator will normally work to take away anything that provides a woman with control and power in her own self to be an independent person. Quite shockingly, this extends to attempting to reduce her spiritual strength too. Of all the types of abuse, this has to be the greatest crime wherein a perpetrator attempts to make his victim lose all hope in Allah ﷻ Himself, and take away her reliance in Allah ﷻ and try to replace it with her being totally dependent upon her perpetrator. He misuses the religion of Allah ﷻ to justify his position and authority over her and therefore her total obedience and submission to him. Yet as we know, Islam means to submit ourselves to Allah ﷻ Alone, full complete submission. This submission should only extend to Allah ﷻ and not to any other being.

We also know that a man is bound to fulfil his responsibilities towards his wife by the profound act of having undertaken a marriage contract with Allah ﷻ Himself. These responsibilities need to be exercised with great care and diligence. It is well known that the man who does not provide the basic food, shelter and clothing for his wife while he has the means is oppressing her. Oppression does not stop there for it extends to the man who makes false promises to his wife, treats her like a slave rather than as a human being who is the daughter of another person, allows others to invade her privacy, and allows his own family members to mistreat and disrespect her.[8] This is the level of diligence required in fulfilling his responsibilities towards her, she is not an object that 'belongs to him', to do with as he pleases. She is her own person free to worship Allah ﷻ. No human has the right to expect and demand total and complete submission and obedience from another human being in the way that Allah ﷻ demands it of His servants.

A perpetrator may also have attempted to play severe psychological games misusing religion as his grounds. Many women new to the religion or who are just beginning to learn about their faith and become more practising, are easy targets. They can be fed a twisted version of the faith especially with access to knowledge being controlled by the perpetrator. Many perpetrators will psychologically torture their victims using their past as a 'valid' argument if the victim was previously of a different or non-faith background or had made known mistakes in her past. Perpetrators psychologically take their victim back into her past and do not allow her to come out of that time in her life via the use of constant reminders and degradation and guilt trips. This can lead a victim into having serious doubts about herself and her faith and thus even provoke her to leaving the version of the faith he has now presented to her as being the only version.

If she is able to escape with her faith intact, the after effects are still profound. She will have many questions in her head, much guilt and burden that is not hers, weighing her down. This may be further exacerbated by family and community members and leaders advising her to be 'patient' and go back to her husband because they have not fully understood the situation and dynamics of abusive relationships. In some cases hearing this, after having literally escaped, can cause a mental breakdown or great loss in faith even though the victim has now left the relationship. Society has just served to prove that her

---

8 Ismail Menk, 2012

abusive husband was right and she was wrong and now all the doors of hope have been closed on her leaving her in total and utter darkness.

In the most tragic of cases, a victim may take her own life where he has made her lose all hope of Mercy and Hope from Allah ﷻ. I pose the question – what evil does a man commit in order to make a woman feel she has no other recourse but to take her own life? What has he brutally stolen from her? What poison has he planted in her mind?

Where a victim is able to gain or regain control of a healthy understanding of her faith, she now has many new battles to deal with. In her recovery process, traditional society expects her to be a woman fulfilling her responsibilities yet at the same time she now has to be a man and fulfil those male responsibilities too, particularly where children are concerned. When she fails to keep both up, she is at great risk of then being looked down upon and frowned upon, by everyone ranging from family, friends, neighbours and community leaders and even establishments that are supposedly there to help her – the very people whom she assumed she would be able to lean on for understanding and support. Additional cultural expectations only serve to add more burdens that have already become unbearable. Once again victims have to face the prejudice that they are away from the perpetrator now so they should be able to function normally, with no consideration for the fact that they may no longer understand what they believe and are too afraid to voice this to anyone.

For a victim who is unable to gain a healthy understanding of what their faith permits and does not, it can cause them to go the other way where they totally repress everything they are feeling and assume what others tell them – that they are being impatient and ungrateful for not getting on with their lives now that they are free from the perpetrator. They therefore drive themselves forward and continue with daily life due to guilt, totally neglecting themselves and their needs except for the bare minimum. Eventually they will either breakdown or totally burn out with all of their symptoms now having built up into medical conditions whether physical or psychological, and thus requiring a more severe degree of intervention.

Chapter 8

IMPACT ON CHILDREN AND PARENTING

Discussing the impact of domestic abuse on children really needs a book of its own in order to do it justice. The impact on children of what they have seen and witnessed cannot be underestimated. One of the most tragic aspects is that children are innocent to all the subtle tactics and games that cannot even be identified by adults as being abusive due to their deadly stealth, so how are children meant to be able to distinguish between what is healthy and what is not? These children will then grow up and be the future generation. In the short term, they are not to be faulted for 'taking sides' and partnering with their father against their mother due to his manipulation and deception – something that would break the heart of any mother. In cases of more visible abuse and aggression, although it is easier to identify right and wrong, it still does not leave the child without some damaging impression on their young minds.

Children require guidance and stability in their lives; the two things that are normally taken away from them whilst living in a household where domestic abuse is happening. As is naturally ingrained in every mother, she would attempt to protect her children and still give them a healthy upbringing as much as she is able. However, when the conditions under which you can be the mother you wish to be are all unhealthy, a mother is totally limited in how much of a healthy upbringing she can in reality provide for her children and how much protection she can give them. This is the hardest thing for a woman to accept once she has left the situation, particularly that she is not to blame and that she did the best she could for survival. It was not her fault that he imposed the unhealthy boundaries within which the family had to operate and she was required to adapt her parenting in order to not risk her children and herself. It is also one of the most challenging things to try and explain to children or outsiders.

Both children and mothers need to invest time into becoming children and mothers again out of the abusive household. It will be very different to how it was during their time in an abusive household. For different age groups there will be differing needs. However, in general, all involved will need to learn what healthy relationships are, what healthy boundaries are and what basic human decency and respect within families is. Accountability and consequences of actions and behaviour is also an area that will need instilling and development in positive rather than destructive ways. In most cases just learning basic right from wrong will sadly also be required.

In many cases, children will often show medical symptoms or conditions such as bed-wetting or eating disorders, or behavioural issues at school as a result of the abuse they are witnessing at home and the trauma this is causing them. Some of these will clear up pretty soon after they are no longer being exposed to the abuse and others will take longer to unlearn and then replace with more healthy behaviours. In some cases, additional professional help may be required.

This is in essence just the tip of the iceberg with regards to children and the aftermath that victims of domestic abuse are left to deal with, usually on their own or with very limited support.

WHY DO WOMEN STAY?

This is the biggest single question that a victim is too often 'accused' of. It is also a perfect way to destroy any sense of hope and ambition a victim has for rebuilding her life as well as validating to her that she was in the wrong and it was all her fault for staying.

Understanding why women stay can be highly complex or it can also be very simple given how you choose to look at it. The overall answer is simple: she stayed because she had no choice. The complexities and variations in this lie in the details of what made her have no choice.

To gain some understanding of the matter it requires looking into the actual cycle of abuse[9] and tied in with that, one of the most basic human needs for companionship and friendship, a sense of belonging and feeling loved. This feeling is innate within each and every one of us and is not something we have the right to point accusatory fingers at others for having, when we ourselves have this very need. The cycle of abuse seeks to exploit that very vulnerable human need. Perpetrators tend to be very alert on the 'weaknesses' which are in effect just basic human needs of their victim and play on this to their advantage regardless of how it hurts the victim. Further to this they may also know additional information about the victim with which they maintain a hold over the victim.

---

9   Lenore Walker, 1979

The cycle of abuse is one wherein a period of calm is followed by uneasiness in the air which only the victim can sense. There is a sense of foreboding that anytime soon an incident is going to kick off. The incident will then indeed take place; it does not need a specific trigger factor. A perpetrator can make absolutely anything into a trigger factor, using it as an excuse. This is absolutely crucial to understand because it means that regardless of what the victim does, there is no escaping an incident. He will ensure it happens despite all her efforts to ensure she is complying with his rules. Once the incident has taken place the perpetrator will attempt to 'win her back' either through guilt trips or through kind treatment. This winning her back is in actual fact his re-establishment of his control upon her because in his eyes she stepped out of line and he needs to once again exert his control back upon her. For someone who continuously goes through this cycle and finds that her spouse is not just nice, but amazingly so during his 'making up' period, she will naturally cling onto this and in her mind it will give her some hope that he may change. Any sign of kind treatment will bring enormous amounts of relief for her that cannot be understated. This is then followed by the calm period once again wherein his rules are re-established, though loitering in the background is unhappiness that 'she pushed him' to the incident by rebelling against whatever he deemed his rules to be, and thus not being the obedient wife he demands. And so the cycle persists. Regardless of what she does she will never be able to meet his unreasonable expectations. With each incident he will be drawing her into a deeper emotional connection to him, exploiting her human needs and most likely her innate desire to make her marriage work, thus making it harder for her to leave.

In addition to this, there may other more tangible reasons why women do not leave abusive relationships straightaway or ever. These can range from being totally isolated, no one she can confide in who will believe her and she can trust, having no safe place she can go to, having no financial independence or even access to any finances at all. She may be caught in the trap of wanting to give her children a family unit, not wanting for them to come from a 'broken home' and the stigma that society and communities can attach to her and her children should she leave. For others it is that they try to leave but time and again they are drawn back into the cycle of abuse by his persuasive heart-rending pleas during the 'making up' phase, or that they are physically pursued by him and family members so that wherever they go, they in essence cannot escape. Spying and lack of any privacy is also something that a lot of victims sadly identify with thus making leaving or the prospects after leaving totally unviable. In other cases it may be the sheer terror he has instilled within her that he most certainly will kill her or the children or cause them serious harm if she even thinks about leaving.

For someone in an abusive relationship, the safest place for her is actually beside the perpetrator. This is a means of survival that victims will realise, whether consciously or subconsciously, and conform to for their own survival and because they see no other way out. It is because of this very reason that if there is much contact with outsiders, the abuse will not be visible because the victim will have aligned herself beside her perpetrator out of fear and lack of choice. The other element to this is that perpetrators will rarely be abusive in front of anyone who may potentially be a threat to them, and they will go the extra mile to ensure that their public reputation is spotless. This makes it even more difficult for a victim to then take a stand against him, especially when he has isolated her from society including family and friends. It may even be that she is made to seem like an unhealthy wife or mother due to the psychological and emotional signs of the abuse now showing on her.

In one way or another, she could not leave because she was trapped. Therefore you cannot accuse a victim of 'having stayed' when she had no choice in the matter thus making the question of asking victims 'why did you stay?' redundant. If we need to ask that, it means we need to increase our understanding of domestic abuse.

Helping the Oppressed

Like a tornado you slowly brewed
Around the edges of my life
Working your way in, subtly at first
Stealthily not leaving anything untouched
You expanded your ruthless gales
Enveloping everything of my life
Spinning it relentlessly around you
Increasing the speed, the ferocity, the rawness
Cutting me up into shreds
Sucking me in so deeply, suffocating me
Until every part of me became baseless
Revolving around you ceaselessly
With no end in sight
Except the ever apparent
Expansion of your hollow core.

You showed no conscience
Mercilessly tearing down
Everything in your path
You would have remained
And long continued your ruthlessness
Except that with your greed for expansion
The end was inevitable
For little was left to devour
Thus your powers receded
And into the darkness you disappeared.

What did you leave behind?
That you cared not to even glance back
Destruction
Total chaos and disorder
Where to start picking up the pieces?
The task ahead overwhelming
The shock numbing
The silence deafening
The heart speechless
For some pain, there are no words.

You uprooted every tree
Every plant, every seed
You shattered every thing of substance
You tore apart walls of safety and security
You exposed warmth to bitter cold
You created a great flurry of activity
Seemingly making you important
But you revealed what you thought was hidden
Your cold and empty core.

You cared not what you did
Perhaps you never will
But the earth holds warmth
Encourages growth, feeds souls
And amongst the chaos
Has the potential for new life.

Chapter 1

LEAVING
DOMESTIC ABUSE

A victim who has finally been able to leave the abusive situation and maybe even finally had her divorce through is still lying on the floor, curled up into a ball, shaking and shivering. Whether or not we understand it, she needed to leave that marriage for her own sanity as just a start. Just because the perpetrator is no longer immediately present does not mean she is alright and can jump up and get on with her life. Her head is reeling with a million emotions and thoughts. The last thing on her mind is getting up. Where she needed help before, she needs even more help now. Without this help and support the chances of her getting up again are very slim. You cannot advise such a person to be 'patient' and expect that they will miraculously stand up again.

Much work is being done to help victims, but sadly the demand for this work outweighs the provision. Each one of us can help to reduce that demand by fulfilling our role as a human being and a citizen with fellow human beings who may require our help and support.

Mention must be made of two of the biggest issues women who have left domestic abuse face. The first is regarding those women who have children, as the majority do tend to. Within communities they are often left to fend for themselves and raise their children single-handedly. They receive plenty of criticism when things go wrong but little recognition or support when achievements or progress is made. As a whole, everyone needs to be made aware that we all have a responsibility towards supporting the youth of today to develop into healthy adults of tomorrow. That means that a key area that all children need to see and experience and be part of is positive role models, both male and female, but male in particular for children who have lived in abusive households.

They need to learn the respect for humans and women in particular that faith teaches us, and see that being lived out in daily life by those around them. They need to see examples of healthy relationships so that they can learn these for their own future. They need to see decency and respect so they can see that the world is much bigger than what they were use to. They need to see honour and accountability so that they know how to live in a balanced and healthy way and make informed life decisions as they grow and develop. If we are not actively doing this and involving children in these vital processes then we too are failing these children further. We cannot leave it all up to the mother to do alone. We have a collective responsibility within society for the future generations. This brings us onto the second point.

Women, whilst they were married, were expected to conform to being in what is perceived as a generally female role. Yet all of a sudden, now she is increasingly vulnerable due to being single, with the responsibility of raising children alone on her shoulders and dealing with the aftermath of abuse, she is then expected by society as a whole to take on the male role as well. She is expected to be the bread winner or be independent and able to look after herself and her children with once again, only faults and mistakes pointed out, rather than encouragement and support for the milestones she has achieved on a daily basis. She is expected to be totally fine and get on with life as normal yet her world has just been crushed to pieces. She is expected to be both the mother and the father despite the fact that the father was clearly unfit to fulfil his responsibilities, yet somehow there is an undercurrent that this was her fault when it clearly was not.

There is one very simple thing for the rest of us to do; that is to actively be there and be a role model in ourselves, yet this is something lacking for women coming out of domestic abuse.

The areas that will be addressed further are testimony to the experiences of victims who have come out of domestic abuse situations and are then faced with a barrage of further barriers to overcome in society.

Chapter 2

ROLE OF FAMILY AND FRIENDS

Whatever relation she may have to you, a person who has gone through domestic abuse that you know of personally, can truly excel in their recovery if you are there to support her. She is cold and in shock; provide her with warmth and affection, ensure her basic needs are met, give her a hug, a continued presence, a reassurance that you are there and are not going to disappear on her, that she is safe.

Going back to her being curled up on the floor, she needs to learn that she can stretch her legs again; reassure her, give her support from which she will find strength to look up, to gather her thoughts a little bit, to move her toes and eventually feel crippled by laying curled up so that she actually needs to stretch. It is as simple as being there, listening, not judging, being a solid and true fellow human being. It is your continued solidarity, support, reassurance, kind words, affection and non judgmental attitude that will enable her to stand on her own two feet again, albeit with you holding her arm.

She will be dizzy as she stands, her head spinning, not knowing how to focus, endless thoughts and emotions going round in her heart and mind. Give her something to hold onto in addition to your support. Call upon whatever other support is available. It is not a sign of weakness to get help, rather it takes courage to ask for and accept help. Nor is it a sign of impatience for we were not created as angels, we were created as humans with humans emotions and needs. The patience here for the victim is to not lose hope and use whatever halal means Allah ﷻ has put at our disposal to help her get back on her feet, whatever the situation may be, and thereafter put our trust in Allah ﷻ after having taken those means. The more options she has to hold onto the more upright she will be able to stand. With this support in place, she will then be able to take those baby steps towards recovery.

She will have many injuries, most of which cannot be seen with the naked eye, but which can be overcome given that help. Do not isolate her at any stage of her journey and you will speed up her ability to take those steps. You may need to hold her hand for a while but at some point she will let go and start walking freely again until eventually she will have the capacity to run. Your support will have given this victim her life back. Do not underestimate just how far the tiniest of actions can go. Your patience is in providing this support. Allah ﷻ will not cease to help you in your own affairs as long as you are helping your fellow humans in need.

The Messenger of Allah ﷺ said, **"Whoever fulfils the needs of his brother, then Allah will fulfil his needs."** [10]

Hence the reality is that you need to support her for her sake as much as for your own. When you have the opportunity to help a victim of oppression, it is just that – an opportunity for you to gain good and get the help of Allah ﷻ in your own life. It is a blessing for you, should you choose to take it, without losing the focus that your deeds are for the pleasure of our Creator alone. As mentioned, you do not have to do it alone either. You can enlist the help of others to make it more manageable in cases where the victim needs high levels of support.

---

10 Part of longer hadith, Sahih Bukhari, hadith number 622

A key area where family and friends often go wrong is in asking questions that seem accusatory towards the victim and blameworthy, as though it was her fault and she did something wrong. This includes asking her 'why did you stay?' as mentioned previously. Although this just demonstrates that such a person has not understood how the cycle of abuse works or what the victim has been through, it will only serve to push the victim away from you, if not cut off from you altogether. She has had enough judgements passed on every aspect of her life, she does not need you to add to it and will instantly protect herself from anything that may seem threatening or remind her of the perpetrator. The real problem with this, however, is that by asking such questions and making such suggestions that she could have done things differently, it will spark a potentially very dangerous cycle off in her head where everything the perpetrator put her through is now being questioned in a self blaming way. Now that she is hearing similar things from outsiders it will lead her to question whether or not he was actually right and therefore was it actually her fault. If a victim becomes stuck in this destructive cycle, it can takes years to get out of it, if at all.

The reality is that all family and friends need to do is be empathic and non judgmental, provide her with company and reduce her isolation, show her what healthy relationships are, be trustworthy and reliable, encourage her to be herself with gentle reminders of all her positive traits and abilities and finally, remind her that she now has a positive future to build. If she receives this consistently from a solid group around her, then she will soon find her strength and grounding again.

Her life will of course never be the same again. However, at least she can build a positive future that she wants to live, being who she truly is.

Chapter 3

ROLE OF COMMUNITY MEMBERS

Collectively as communities we need to initiate more programmes that demonstrate care about other members of our community and reduce isolation for those who have limited or no family and friends. There needs be a central hub of activities in every community that anyone and everyone can be welcomed to and freely participate in and that encourages caring for others and providing trustworthy support.

Community members can play a similar role as family and friends to victims of domestic abuse when they know about it. When they do not know about it, they can individually and collectively work on being a role model and setting an example to others in their conduct, concern for others, non judgmental attitudes, not interfering in things that are not their business, and not imposing cultural preferences on others especially over religious obligations and recommendations. The more people that take pride in building a true community, the more encouraging it will be for others to follow their example. The more individuals do this, the easier it will be for victims to integrate back into society - a skill they will have to re-learn and feel safe in doing so.

Communities also need to champion causes that are set up to provide professional and essential help to victims of domestic abuse. These are over-subscribed and need as much support as possible. In whatever way communities can come together to support such organisations, then they are contributing to saving the lives of the most vulnerable on their very doorstep. We often rush to help the needy abroad, and rightly so, human suffering anywhere needs to be alleviated. This, however, needs to be done in a balanced way by ensuring those in need locally are also looked after. The consequences long term of not doing this is that we are looking at a future where there will be fewer and fewer people to help those abroad let alone locally, as manageable problems become epidemics because they were not dealt with and instead were brushed under the carpet as 'someone else's problem'.

Chapter 4

ROLE OF COMMUNITY LEADERS

Community leaders who find themselves caught in between a victim and a perpetrator admittedly hold a difficult position. Given the right understanding of the subject area though, as with other sciences, there is always a procedure to be followed for different circumstances. Each situation you are asked to assist in will need to be dealt with on an individual basis and what may apply in some situations will not be appropriate for others.

There are certain things, however, that should be avoided or one should be aware of as a community leader and these have been summarised as follows:

> If a victim approaches you without the knowledge of her husband and she expresses great fear of what he may do to her if he was to know she had told anyone about the abuse, then that is an indication of high levels of danger. It may or may not be safe for her to go back to him depending on the context of her approaching you, i.e. whether she is asking you to help and wants to remain in the marriage or whether she has fled because it has become too unbearable and dangerous.

> For a victim to reach out and tell someone about the abuse, means she has exhausted all other possible means and is now getting desperate if not already beyond desperate. It is not the time to

be told to be patient. Her patience has been stretched beyond the limit. This type of advice could put her life at risk.

> Oppressive actions that are clearly labelled as such and condemned by those who hold authority and leadership within the community will help a victim to understand and come to terms with the fact that she was wronged. This will aid her recovery process significantly and reduce any destructive guilt that has been wrongly imposed upon her. It will also help her to understand her religion better and make sense of it within her heart from a faith context. By clearly stating to her that she has been wronged, you are restoring some faith back into her heart as well as defending the religion of Allah ﷻ.

> In cases where clear and high levels of oppression are being inflicted on the wife and where divorce is the only option left, community leaders need to help facilitate this process. Many victims have door after door shut on them with refusals to help her in getting her husband to release her from the marriage, which has in reality been long dead. She is thus left hanging with no way out and no way forward. Often she is left alone to face this battle via long, drawn-out and costly processes for which she does not have the mental strength nor the financial means. This is further oppression added to everything she has already been through and every effort needs to be exerted into minimising this in ways that are clearly permitted within Islam. There should be no fear associated with upholding the laws of Allah ﷻ in preventing oppression. As long as a victim is tied to the perpetrator by some legal means, she will not be able to be completely free of his oppression.

These are just some of the key factors that come up time and again. It is not possible to go into extensive detail of how to deal with each individual case, as each case will differ given the context. The more community leaders that have an in depth understanding of the area of domestic abuse and all the sensitivities it involves, then the better equipped they will be to deal with cases as they arise. It is hoped other chapters within this book will assist in gaining some of that understanding.

Chapter 5

ROLE OF
PERPETRATORS

Perpetrators have the greatest responsibility towards victims. However, at the same time, they are most probably going to have the least contact with the victim if she has left him.

As a perpetrator you need to first and foremost understand your wrongdoing and as will be discussed further, change your ways and make that sincere request for forgiveness. This includes correcting all of the wrongs that you have committed. It may sound like a daunting task and the reality is that for some of the oppression you have inflicted, you will struggle to make amends. However, it is better faced while you are still able to do something about it, rather than it going with you on your account of deeds, in the grave and before Allah ﷻ on the Day of Judgement.

You will need to examine every area, emotional, physical, psychological, sexual, financial and spiritual and be brutally honest with yourself in what you need to do to make up whatever oppression you inflicted in each area and actually take active measures to carry out those actions.

The reality is that until you seek that forgiveness and truly regret what you have done, you will forever be walking around with those deeds on your shoulders. They will not disappear just because you choose to ignore them. Worse than that is that your oppression will then return to haunt you on the Day of Judgement and be darkness for you in return for the darkness you inflicted in this life. Do you really want that? On the other hand, as long as you still have life left within you, you can always seek that true change. You can remove that darkness in both worlds.

Some victims will want to know of your change and your willingness to make amends, but that does not mean they necessarily want to be with you ever again or indeed see you ever again. You will have to accept that. Other victims will never want to hear anything about you ever again. That is something you cannot do anything about and should not attempt to either.

However the victim chooses to respond to you, or if she chooses to not permit you anywhere near her, you shall have to accept that as a direct consequence of your actions and still do whatever is within your means to make amends without antagonising the situation or causing her any further harm. It is not being recommended to get in touch with her directly here, but for you to use some logic and common sense in how you make amends.

The Messenger of Allah ﷺ said, **"Beware of injustice, for oppression will be darkness on the day of resurrection."**[11]

---

11 Sahih Bukhari, Book of Oppressions, hadith number 8

Chapter 6

ROLE OF VICTIMS

Finally, of course victims do have some responsibility towards themselves for their own healing and recovery, and how they deal with the aftermath of all they have been through. This will be explored in detail in 'Section 5: On the Road to Recovery'.

SECTION 4

Helping the Oppressor

Narrated Anas 🙠, Allah's Messenger ﷺ said:
"Help your brother, whether he is an oppressor
or he is an oppressed one. People asked,
"O Allah's Messenger! It is all right to help him
if he is oppressed, but how should we help him
if he is an oppressor?" The Prophet said,
"By preventing him from oppressing others."[12]

---

12 Sahih Bukhari, hadith number 624

Chapter 1

A COLLECTIVE OBLIGATION

In our own way, each and every one of us has a role to play in helping oppressors stop their oppression. This may be through direct or indirect means. The indirect ways are clear cut, first and foremost being that we examine our own lives and ensure we are living in a way whereby we are not inflicting oppression on anyone in any way, shape or form. Secondly, it is by ensuring that wherever we see oppression whatever form it may be in, we stand up against it even if only verbally to condemn it. It is important that both of these are done hand in hand. It is no good doing one and not the other.

Even if we are confident that we are not oppressing anyone, it does no harm to merely reflect over our lives and our relationships and interaction with different people and assess ourselves. If we can take that confidence to certainty, then that only protects ourselves. And if we find that we do need to change some of our behaviours, then once again we have actually just protected ourselves and others also in the process. In addition to this, we also need to ensure our guards are on alert and we do not let them slip in future, in both of these scenarios. If each and every one of us were to do this sincerely for the sake of Allah ﷻ, imagine the amount of oppression that would be removed from the earth.

For those who are more ingrained in their ways, the more people that stand up to oppression then the harder it becomes for them to continue with such actions. It is sadly the silence which allows, in many ways, the oppression and suffering to continue presently and into the future. This is where the direct means come into play and which will be addressed further.

One point to note in this is that attention will be drawn to problem areas, not to show up faults or point fingers, but as a means to show the areas that collectively and individually need working on for the betterment of all. There are many success stories out there of positive work being done and these need to continue. At the same time there is much further work that needs to be carried out in a sensitive but effective manner.

Chapter 2

'RESPONSIBILITY OF COMMUNITY 'LEADERS

Community leaders are more likely to be aware of situations where domestic abuse is occurring as they are more likely to be approached for help in such matters in confidence. This is no easy task but it is not impossible.

There are two elements to this, firstly how do community leaders deal with each situation effectively and secondly, how do community leaders pave the way for the members of their community to live with basic safety, respect and humanity that is free from such oppression?

With regards to dealing with individual cases of domestic abuse, the simple answer is that unless a person truly understands a problem then they essentially cannot do much about it and in fact, they can actually cause harm by attempting to do good. We understand this ethos from the Messenger of Allah ﷺ. Therefore community leaders need to ensure they have a proper understanding of the issue of domestic abuse and the intricacies it involves first and foremost. This may be done via professional training, speaking to professionals in the field, speaking to leaders of other communities who have a positive track record of dealing with such problems and reading into the area and the like. Thus one of the reasons behind this book is to make that knowledge more accessible and beneficial, insha'Allah. There are many options out there but community leaders must be willing to learn about those methods and then seek that expertise to help them in dealing effectively with such cases. Once they are equipped with the knowledge then that means they will have more insight at their disposal that will have a positive impact without causing either the victim or the perpetrator, or anyone else, any harm.

Community leaders have the advantage of being able to speak quite frankly and directly to perpetrators once they know of the situation. This is an extremely important and valuable asset that community leaders have at their disposal which should not be overlooked. How many women have been left hanging or imprisoned in a marriage with their physical and mental well-being at stake because where individuals potentially could have changed the course of the situation, they instead did little and remained quiet. Community leaders can potentially have a greater impact on the perpetrator than anyone else, especially if no one else knows about it. The more regularly they can monitor and call the perpetrator to account for his actions, then the more difficult it will be for him to continue the abuse. Most community leaders will be viewed as having such a leadership role because of their knowledge and practice from a religious perspective. This must be utilised to help the perpetrator truly understand the consequences of their actions, not only in this life, but also in the hereafter without any cultural slants or variations, just straight cut from clear religious sources. Procedures for ending marriages based on religious grounds can also be followed through in cases where it becomes necessary with no other recourse, via community leaders.

Of course it is not that simple and straightforward. However, if perpetrators feel that they could lose their marriage due to their actions from a higher authority than themselves then that will force them to sit up and pay heed. Instead, it has been known for perpetrators to feel justified in their actions because the issue has been addressed from a cultural perspective rather than with the clear cut religious evidences that state in no ambiguous terms that such oppression is not permitted. The majority of community leaders will understand where such things have crept in and whatever they can do to help others within their circles to gain a better understanding of how to deal with such problems, then the more people and communities will benefit.

With regards to the second issue of paving the way for community members to live in safety and without fear within their homes, each and every institution, mosques in particular, should be willing to set an example to others and lead the way in proactively addressing this issue. Many institutions often wait for others for the fear of backlash or so as not to be seen as 'breaking the mould' or being 'too outrageous'. Helping to potentially save lives and improve lives is not being outrageous. The longer people wait for others to take the first step, the worse the problem will become until eventually it becomes unmanageable.

The other common fear that arises is that of fearing that Islam will be given a bad name if such an issue is brought to light so that it can be tackled. We need to realise that by not tackling the issue we are just brushing domestic abuse, which is actually prevalent in all communities regardless of religion, under the carpet and when things eventually do get set alight, it will be a very big fire that will then most definitely cause damage. Hence these fears will be realised when they did not need to be. Pretending the problem is not there will not make it go away. Dealing with it head on means we can actually attempt to take some control over it and set a positive example to others.

Collectively there also needs to be concentrated effort on the core fundamentals of what makes a healthy society and a healthy individual in that society, with focus on respect for humanity and women, fulfilment of responsibilities rather than demands of rights, and continuous striving for personal improvement for that higher purpose in life. If the leading institutions within the communities are caught up in arguments over technical issues, building projects and groups and divisions, then the community is essentially held back from development of any kind. The common ground that we all share needs to be utilised rather than cast aside to the detriment of all.

Chapter 3

RESPONSIBILITY
OF COMMUNITY
MEMBERS

Communities must be able to stand together in solidarity to show what we will and will not accept within our fold. The more education and awareness there is around the different forms of oppression and how it will not be tolerated, then the less likely it is to happen in that community.

Each and every member of a community must also stand together in demonstrating the best of characteristics to everyone and really look out for each other and what others may be in need of. This is simply having respect, care and consideration for the humanity of others and is something we should instil in ourselves first and foremost, then our families, our young, elders and everyone within our social circle.

Communities normally only tend to become aware of domestic abuse situations when something goes very wrong; it may even be that the victim has tragically lost her life. This requires us to be reactive in terms of showing disapproval and zero tolerance, without of course resorting to violence or illegal means. From that we must also more importantly, take measures to be proactive in order to ensure the future protection of community members from such horrific situations. There may also be extended family members of the perpetrator who require support and help in coming to terms with what has happened, who have nothing to do with his actions but are caught up in the aftermath of them.

It is no good taking the stance that it is someone else's problem. If it happened to another human being then it is our problem collectively and the closer to us it is, the more responsibilities we have. Whatever can be done collectively to show perpetrators in a legal manner that there is no room for such behaviour in this community, will allow for a very powerful message to be sent to anyone who considers it to be acceptable to behave that way.

Chapter 4

RESPONSIBILITY OF FAMILY AND FRIENDS

Perpetrators need to be shown clear consistent disapproval for their actions. If this comes from immediate family and friends then this makes it more difficult for him to continue about his business without acknowledging his actions. By default, he will be forced to address his behaviour and actions if everyone around him is reminding him and demonstrating that he cannot behave in such a manner and that it is simply unacceptable. When this is not done, that is when it gives him the green light to continue in his ways. This can be done without putting yourself at risk of harm; that is not being recommended here.

Of course in order for family and friends to be able to do this, they must firstly know about what he is doing. This is where it is important that we educate ourselves and learn to read the signs, as well as just generally look out for each other and ensure that if there are signs for concern, we do not just ignore them, nor do we probe to a degree that is completely intrusive. Instead we can enquire in a concerned and reassuring manner and just have that extra alertness and be there to help if anyone does need to confide in us.

If perpetrators do come to us seeking help, then in such instances we should not abandon them. If they are genuine in wanting to change themselves then we can potentially save a life by helping them, whether it may be their own or that of someone else. The more consistent and sensible people they have in their lives that they can turn to and that can help and assist them, the more likely they are to be successful in changing themselves.

It is vital however, you remember that you are not there to pass judgements and present your own views and opinions on the issues that are raised. Islam makes it clear regarding oppression. Do not look for excuses and arguments. Instead simply help the individual to be a better Muslim and better human being. You do not have the right to look down upon the perpetrator or indeed the victim, nor do you have the right to judge and condemn him and his future. It is only the actions we have the right to condemn and not the person, for every human has the potential to change. If you can help then do so, if you cannot stop yourself from giving your personal 'input' then it is better for you stay out of it for you may very well end up being an oppressor yourself to the perpetrator. The purpose in helping a perpetrator is to assist him to change without harming yourself in the process whether in the immediate future or more importantly, in the hereafter.

Chapter 5

ROLE OF THE VICTIM

Who would possibly think that the victim has any role to play in putting a stop to the oppression? The reality is that victims do have a role to play. It has been called a 'role' as opposed to a responsibility in the case of victims because in a lot of cases, the victim may be at a psychological and emotional level where they cannot take this on as a responsibility and it would not be healthy or fair to expect them to do so. Therefore for those who are able, it is a role that they can choose to participate in, to whatever level they are capable. These roles are quite simple. However, the realistic manifestations of them may not be quite so simple.

Whilst in the situation the victim, as much as she is able, can remind their perpetrator of his accountability to Allah ﷻ even if this is done in an indirect way, without any reference to the abuse. For many, to make reference to the abuse would potentially exacerbate it, if not put their lives at risk. Each individual will know for sure what the best approach is for them.

Within the actual situation itself, there is very little else the victim can do without risking her life or increasing the danger to her and any children. It is important that both the victim and others understand and accept this. Not doing so only leads to imposing further guilt upon the victim which she does not need to feel and is not responsible for, and can harm her mental state even more.

Therefore that only leaves one other option; that is to leave the oppression so that the oppression can no longer physically take place. A victim, and indeed everyone else, needs to accept and understand that by leaving the oppression she is actually doing the perpetrator a great favour for it makes him unable to access her and therefore continue the same oppression. This is especially true if he shows no signs of remorse or change and much time has passed, or the situation only seems to be getting worse with time. In her leaving, he may attempt to continue the oppression via other prolonged harassment methods as is common, but it cannot be to the same level by default because he cannot physically access his victim any longer.

It must be brought to attention that the most dangerous time for a victim of domestic abuse is actually at the time of her attempting to leave.[13] This is when her life is at the most risk and therefore attempts to leave must be carried out very carefully and preferably planned in advance with the help of others. As is often the case though, many find themselves in a situation where they have to leave immediately otherwise that will be the very end of their life and thus it is spontaneous without any pre-planning. Both are equally as dangerous.

For victims, it needs to be stressed that you do not need to feel guilty for having left an oppressive husband. You are doing him a favour as it will lessen his account in terms of how much oppression he inflicted upon you when he stands before Allah ﷻ. You have in effect acted as much as you can upon the sunnah to prevent him from carrying out his oppression by leaving.

Readers may be wondering why there is the sudden jump from reminders of accountability within the situation to leaving

---

13 Lees, 2000

the situation with no middle ground. The reason is because we are potentially dealing with saving lives in the case of domestic abuse and therefore we should not be doing anything that can possibly put that life at risk. By having a middle ground where people are involved and become aware of the abuse and try to speak to the perpetrator on behalf of his wife, it only increases the risk of the abuse escalating. It thus becomes important to fully understand what kind of situations we are referring to, for we know that within Islam disputes between the spouses are recommended to be sorted out with middlemen or mediators who try to encourage the disputing parties to meet in the middle or restore each other's rights. Such mediation is possible where people are just temperamental and have certain character flaws within themselves which they need to improve and work on. These could be called disputes.

In the case of a husband who is a serious perpetrator of domestic abuse, that is, it has continued for a significant period of time or is very intense abuse over a short period of time and spans different elements of the types of abuse and what areas they can take place within, is very different to someone who has a character flaw and inflicts oppression and abuse upon his wife but then given a confrontation by either herself or an outsider, regrets and reforms himself. The two scenarios are very different and we need to distinguish between the two.

In this case we are not referring to the latter, instead we are referring to those cases where the spouse truly is a deeply rooted perpetrator if not a serial perpetrator. He has in effect committed a crime. In such cases mediation can put the life of the wife at risk and more than likely, if she has not already attempted mediation and faced the backlash of her attempts from her husband, he most certainly would have made it clear to her what the consequences would be if she ever told anyone about what was happening. Therefore there is no possibility of mediation in this situation, either because it has already been attempted or to attempt it, would put the life of the wife and/or children at risk.

One final stage at which the victim can play a role in helping the perpetrator is if he does actually change and somewhere down the line, asks for forgiveness because he has finally realised and understood accountability and his wrongs and genuinely regrets what he has put you through. You can choose to forgive him. This is not the same as saying his actions were justified, or saying that you have not been hurt and are still maybe suffering from the after effects of what he did. All of these can still co-exist with forgiving him. Your forgiveness will not take away what has happened, but it will put some closure on the matter for you both. Your forgiveness may free him to lead a completely different life from which you also may benefit in the hereafter and maybe even in this worldly life. Your forgiveness may help him to stop being an oppressor.

There will be more on the issue of forgiveness in the section 'On the Road to Recovery'.

Chapter 6

RESPONSIBILITY OF THE PERPETRATOR

It is not possible for every person in society to have a responsibility towards helping the perpetrator put an end to his oppression and injustice without, of course, the perpetrator first and foremost taking his own responsibility to help himself.

If a perpetrator does not help himself then any outside help will be limited in benefitting him. All those who help are only trying to protect the perpetrator from having to face the consequences of such oppression when they stand before Allah ﷻ. They are doing the perpetrator a favour. But at the end of the day, when the Last Day does arrive and everyone is standing before Almighty Allah ﷻ, there will be no one then to help anyone else. Each and every person will have to stand and face the consequences of their own actions. My question to every perpetrator – how do you imagine you will stand before Allah ﷻ and raise your eyes let alone answer for inflicting oppression, abuse and torment upon the one with whom you took a contract with Allah ﷻ, promising that you would look after, honour and protect her? How? Is it not weighty enough that we have to answer for everything else we do, yet you want to add these kinds of deeds to your account? Have you not understood Who you are going to stand before? May Allah ﷻ guide us all before it is too late.

As long as you are living in the world it is never too late to make that reformation, but just bear in mind that as you have harmed another human being you will be required to seek their forgiveness and put right your wrongs in order for your repentance to be accepted. That means you need to act fast before their soul or your soul returns to The Creator, for only Allah ﷻ knows how soon that will be.

You should note that the conditions of repentance are as follows:
1. That you have given up the oppression in totality.
2. That you are sincere and deeply regret what you have done.
3. That you vow to stay away from committing those actions ever again and that includes staying away from anything which may lead to those actions.
4. That you restore the rights of the person you have wronged.

If you are truly sincere about changing, then it will be your responsibility to demonstrate the above to the one you are asking for forgiveness from without any clauses of expecting her to return to you, if she has separated from you, or anything else. Your taking responsibility should be a matter of its own. You yourself will know that you may have made these promises many times before and broken them hence if you are met with any cynicism or antagonism in the first instance, then that is only to be expected. Therefore this time, if it is for real then that reality will need to be demonstrated. You should also be prepared to get professional help if that is what you need, if there are other underlying causes of why you have resorted to such ways. On the other hand it may be that you need to get help in re-learning some of the fundamental issues of what it truly means to be a Believer and thereby the kind of conduct we should have with others, particular close and female family members.

If you are afraid that you will not be forgiven then you have begun to understand the enormity of what you put your victim through and therefore the vast amount you need to do in order to restore rights and make amends. These are direct consequences of your actions that are better faced in the worldly life than in the hereafter. Allah ﷻ will be a witness to your efforts and perhaps that will draw His Mercy onto you in untold ways. If you are sincere to Allah ﷻ and true in your regret then you will persist in making amends. That does not mean you harass your ex-victim for forgiveness if she is no longer in your life, but that you do other things to restore her rights and put right the wrongs and perhaps through a third party, draw her attention once to your actions, or leave it with Allah ﷻ to decide. You must understand how much you are asking from her by asking her to forgive you. At the same time, you do not need to despair – a purified heart will shine out.

On the Road to Recovery

From time to time, the tears burst forth
As the grief becomes overwhelming
Deep croaky broken sobs, unexpected.
The heart constricts once again
As faded imprints on the mind resurface
As lost hopes seem to creep out of sight.
Just as suddenly it halts
Leaving behind it the calm after the storm
Fresh winds, lighter air, deep breaths once again.
A peace descends, newfound tranquillity
Relief, calmness, a deep acceptance
Contentment and the gifts it brings.

If a healthy closure was possible with you
I would wish you the best for the future.
I pray your heart softens with mercy
I wish you change and understanding for your own sake
I'm proud of all your achievements in life
You should be too, without the destruction.
A reminder for us all
Success, name and fame may come our way
But blessings used to destruct
Will never rectify wrongs
Those deeds will catch us at the gates of paradise
Perhaps forever blocking our entry.
Reality is, I don't wish that for you
Between you, me and God
We know the truth.
Every day is a chance to put right the wrongs
And strive towards achieving the ultimate character
I wish you the best in that
It's your business now.
I showed you much mercy
Walking away is further mercy for you

For it reduces your oppression.
You will always carry your deeds upon your heart
Travel as you may across the earth
Gaining titles and prestige, name and status.
It will weigh you down
But it is your business now
You have the choice to change.
One day you will stand before God
I pray that day, these deeds will have been rectified
No longer chained to your heart
I pray your conscience tastes the sweetness of liberating yourself.

If a healthy closure was possible
I would wish you well
And tell you to start being who you were born to be
Before your designated time runs out.

Chapter 1

STAGES OF RECOVERY

It is essential to understand that there is a process of recovery for all victims of domestic abuse and that time and consistent support is needed for this to take place.

In his book, 'Why Does He Do That', Lundy Bancroft identifies the three stages of recovery as the following:

1. Establishment of Safety
2. Remembrance and Mourning
3. Reconnection with Ordinary Life

These are expanded on below based on my work with victims of domestic abuse.

ESTABLISHMENT OF SAFETY

In order for victims to even commence the recovery process they need to be out of the abusive situation and away from the perpetrator. There is no chance for any recovery to begin until this happens for the simple reason that a victim has to survive on a daily basis whilst still with the perpetrator. They are not living life; they are simply existing and surviving from one minute to the next due to the abuse, the unspoken rules, and the uncertainty of when the next 'incident' will be. Therefore in order for them to take any steps towards rebuilding themselves, they need that safe environment in which they can do so.

If you have come out of domestic abuse then you need to do the very basics of looking after yourself once again, something you will have been forced to neglect throughout the abuse. This includes ensuring you are sleeping as well as possible. This often can take a long time to settle into due to nightmares and flashbacks and general high levels of anxiety so it may require that you initially sleep at times during the day as well if that is when sleep comes to you, with a view to building a more stable night-time sleeping routine. It also includes eating proper meals at set times, which will help stabilise your moods and emotions as well as ensuring that your body is once again getting the nutrients it needs to keep you healthy. You may wish to consider taking up some light form of exercise or regular gentle walks. It is important to go easy on the body and not do too much all at once. Your body would have suffered from an intense amount of trauma leaving you in a constant state of fight or flight response, with the adrenaline and anxiety on high alert. Your body now needs to learn to come out of that and relax once again and not be so tense, hence easing your way back into things will prevent giving your body a shock that could lead to all sorts of health issues. Take the time to do things that will help you to look after yourself and relax more, whether that is having a regular hot relaxing bath, reading in bed, spending time with fun and light-hearted people, or just contemplating. If you have children, it may also mean spending more quality and fun time with them where you can be your true self and the parent you wish to be.

Once that safety has been established, one of the key things that will assist you more than anything else is to ensure that you are fully alert when praying and are praying with all of yourself present in front of Allah ﷻ as much as is possible. During the abuse the chances of praying with that true dedication and concentration would have been slim due to your every day being about the perpetrator and your survival. You can now reclaim this outlet that will help your recovery process and give you a secret and special stability and understanding and is a gift that you can take pride in. The importance of prayer in your recovery process cannot be emphasised enough. You have been wronged and you should not feel shy to ask Allah ﷻ of your needs whatever they may be; just remember that your prayers will be answered and so you should also ask wisely.

REMEMBRANCE AND MOURNING

The remembrance and mourning is, in essence, the cycle of grief a person experiences when they have lost someone close to them. This may sound odd, considering this person will have left someone who has inflicted harm upon them, but what many of us fail to remember is that the victim is a normal human being who would have had hopes, dreams and wishes at the start of their relationship like many of us naturally do. They would not have known that they would be marrying a perpetrator, for the warning signs can be subtle in most cases or just seem like flattery and male protectiveness or 'gheerah' in the first instance. Therefore a victim will have had the shock of dealing with the fact that this person is not actually who they thought they were firstly, and secondly, the loss of all those hopes and dreams they had for their marriage and partnership with their spouse will be an additional shock. The spouse they thought they had and all the hopes they had have actually 'died', in some cases a sudden death and thus the grieving process now will naturally happen. This is the key area that many of us fail to understand or accommodate and thereby only cause more anguish to victims instead of utilising the opportunity to help.

For those who have gone through this ordeal, you yourself may not recognise that you are grieving except to know that you have unexplained pain and sadness that eats away at you and weighs heavy on your heart but which you cannot explain the reasons for.

The four main emotions related to the grieving cycle are Denial, Anger, Mourning and Acceptance. The denial will partly stem from the shock of realising that the person you married is not really the person you thought they were. It is easier to deny this than accept it. It is also easier to deny any of the abuse or the extent of it because of the emotional attachment you will have formed with your spouse. It will be very hard to accept that in actual fact they hurt you in many ways and treated you in a manner that you will come to understand as degrading and debasing. This is not a reflection of yourself in any way at all; it is instead a reflection of your perpetrator. The pain from this will nevertheless still cut into you and you should realise that is normal for everyone in your shoes.

When we are stripped of our human dignity we cannot help but feel pain, hurt and degradation. The full realisation of this is what then leads onto the feelings of anger and sometimes rage, that not only could another human being resort to such debased treatment but that it was the one person you probably invested the most trust in and expected the most from. Dealing with this rage and anger will be discussed further, later in this chapter.

The mourning is the heavy sadness that will naturally overtake your heart at times when you think about things you have shared, the loss you feel due to the hopes you had, and the good times in amidst the bad times when there were some glimpses of human affection. Every human has been created with the need for companionship so when a person loses the person they thought would accompany them for the rest of their life, it is to be expected that you will feel much sadness.

Finally as you come to terms with everything that you have been through you, will come to accept all that has happened and that your spouse was not who you thought they were. This acceptance will eventually pave the way for you to look forward in your life, towards the future and take the steps required in order to actually tangibly move forward. It will take time but taking the first steps is key to making progress. Without you taking these steps any external help will be limited in how much it can benefit you.

RECONNECTION WITH ORDINARY LIFE

Throughout the remembrance and mourning stage, you would have already been doing normal everyday activities, albeit most likely to a lesser degree. However when you really reconnect with ordinary life you will actively be looking to do new things and enjoy life again. It may take some time and the sadness and grief may still linger but on the whole, the true reconnection is when the acceptance of the past has taken place and you are making the most of the present, with a view to building a future. There may be times when the odd emotion from the mourning stage resurfaces due to memories or incidents and reminders which trigger off past events but you will find that as time passes by, it becomes easier to not only handle these situations but also understand them and be aware of the potential things that may trigger off certain emotions.

Recognising these emotions will help you to take control of your life again and be you again if you choose to do so. It may be daunting at first but given the chance, you may be surprised at the hidden strengths you find within yourself. You do after all now have a bank of human experience behind you. It is vital to remember that your life is now back in your hands and you can channel it to where you wish; you have the choice in this and the responsibility also. You can obviously draw on the help of others, but essentially, the hard work will need to be done by yourself and equally you will gain the rewards of this effort.

Chapter 2

APPROACHING
RECOVERY

For many victims of domestic abuse, if not all, at the beginning of the recovery process it may feel like there will never be any recovery. The path ahead may seem extremely daunting and like a mountain that can never be climbed, but it does not need to be this way and with time you will find that you have amazing capabilities instilled within you and you have the power to allow these to transpire if you have the firm intention to move your life forward and build a new life for yourself. In a lot of ways it is actually an opportunity for you to start afresh and be who you really wish to be and achieve all you wish to achieve in life.

In essence, the recovery process starts with your attitude and feelings towards it. If you decide from the outset that there is no recovery and that life will never be positive again, then you are likely to not move beyond that. If however you can take the courageous step of admitting that life will never be the same again but it does not need to be negative or without positive purpose, that there are things you can achieve and that you can choose to take steps to be happy again, then your success in recovery has already commenced. You have already taken the bravest step of getting out of an oppressive situation in no doubt the most difficult of circumstances. There will still be rough and low days ahead, but in all, you still have a future and you can choose where you channel it. Your perpetrator would have tried to bury your ability to think for yourself and be who you wish to be, but therein lies the key. The real you is still there, just buried in the background and not used to being at the forefront of your life.

Start by making simple choices again; what to eat for your daily meals, what to wear, when to do certain things, how to have your home environment, your favourite colours and so on. You will soon find that you discover you are more than capable of thinking for yourself and making decisions, some of those might be more difficult than others, but it is possible. It always has been possible and this is what threatened your perpetrator hence why he needed to crush down that threat to his control and power. It does not mean that you are in any way a bad individual for having thoughts and wishes about decisions in your life, it just means that you are sensible enough to realise that life is short and decisions need to be made in order to live the most fulfilling life possible. You are in essence taking responsibility for your life and actions and no one can possibly criticise that.

It is also essential that you give yourself the time that you need to heal and for every individual this will be different. You do not need to rush. You can take things at your own pace in order to ensure that you truly have come to terms with things and dealt with all the emotions and pain you have experienced. Taking your time will only contribute to your strength and long term stability and it is not a sign of weakness. You will have your good days and bad days, but as long as you are focussing on building a future rather than living in the past, this is all healthy and part of the recovery process. As mentioned, there will be times when certain triggers take you back into what you have been through. This will gradually get better with time once you realise what these trigger factors are and accept that you are no longer living that life, hence these trigger factors do not need to be associated with your perpetrator any longer. This may take some working on initially and requires you to be honest with yourself and examine the underlying emotions behind these triggers, but in the long term, with a bit of help, they can be turned around so that they no longer have an adverse effect on you or at least do not debilitate you.

Chapter 3

UNDERSTANDING PATIENCE

There are many myths that surround the whole issue of patience or *'sabr'*. Many victims of domestic abuse are often told by family and community members, elders and leaders that they should be patient with their husband and not make him angry. If they manage to get out of the marriage with their lives intact then they are further told that they should be patient in putting up with his unwillingness to cooperate and just give him what he wants to make things easier, not to make things more difficult. They are then left to pick up the pieces of their broken lives and are told to be patient whilst they are totally isolated, with no support, no understanding, no one to talk to and no one to turn to. They are told they should be fine now and be able to get on with their lives because they are no longer living with the perpetrator.

None of this is patience. This is further oppression inflicted on the already oppressed at a crucial time when they are extremely vulnerable. The women themselves will also begin to believe these messages as it is reinforced time and again everywhere they turn.

Allah ﷻ does not tell us that we have to keep silent when we see oppression. Rather we are told the opposite, that we should help both the oppressed and the oppressor by putting an end to his oppression. A woman speaking up about her abusive husband is acting upon this and is an opportunity for the wider community to help stop oppressors in committing further sin that will only lead to darkness on the Day of Judgement. If we are supposed to wish for others what we wish for ourselves, would we not want for each individual to have light on the Day of Judgement rather than a darkness that cannot be described? If communities took a firm stand against such oppression where would it leave room for oppression to continue? The person who looks down upon the woman who has finally spoken out against the oppression of her husband should consider that she is doing him a favour by drawing attention to the fact that he needs help for the sake of his hereafter. It is not patience to put up with such oppression. Patience is to seek whatever help possible and thereafter leave the matter with Allah ﷻ.

Outsiders must bear in mind two things: when a victim speaks out she is not doing so after the first or second incident. She would have most likely suffered much abuse and untold trauma and is only speaking out because she simply cannot cope anymore and things have gotten very much out of hand. Secondly, outsiders need to also understand that a woman who lives in daily fear may not be able to speak up due to the fear she has for either herself or any children. It therefore becomes more incumbent upon outsiders to look out for our fellow community and family members and speak up where there is clear proof that abuse is going on. This of course must be done in a way that the safety of the victim and any children are not compromised.

Many perpetrators will attempt to continue the oppression through various manipulation and control tactics long after the victim has left the marriage, especially where children are concerned. Each case needs to be dealt with individually. However, a key point to remember is that everyone, especially children, are entitled to be protected from those who will harm them, even if that be a parent. A parent does not just automatically have rights to their child if they are violating that child's rights and are a source of harm to that child. We know from history that parents were taken to account for even the names given to children which had bad and harmful meanings during the time of the Prophet ﷺ. So what of a father who even if he is not physically abusive towards a child, plays emotional and psychological games, turning child against mother and sibling against sibling, all in an effort to get continued domination and control? What of the father who neglects the child and financially does not provide for the child? What of the father who uses his child to spy on the mother whom he is no longer married to? These are not times for commanding 'patience', these are times for gaining a proper understanding into each situation and the mentality of abusive individuals and helping them stop their continued attempts at oppression by putting protection, regulation and accountability in place. This not only protects the vulnerable but also protects the perpetrator from inflicting further oppression. Islam is not a man made system. Its rules are from Great Wisdom that is beyond human comprehension. If we followed them, we would come to realise and understand this.

For those women who have to undergo this trauma of learning how to live again, you have not lost out, you have rather gained. You will return to our Creator having been a wronged person, your prayers are accepted without any barrier, Allah ﷻ has taken an oath that He will most assuredly support you even if it be after a while, your sins will be expiated for the pain and suffering you have experienced, you will have gained wisdom and experience that others can never imagine, you have the right to retaliate but by choosing not to you gain forgiveness and can expect reward in the hereafter. These are just some of the gains and they alone are enough to be overwhelming. It does not mean that the oppression and suffering you were under was justified, not at all. But it does mean you have the upper hand. Would you rather face Allah ﷻ as the oppressor with all of his dark deeds on his account? Or would you rather face Allah ﷻ as the oppressed where your rights were taken away from you yet you chose not to retaliate?

In the recovery process, you should note that others may be there to hold your hand and support you, but they cannot hold all of your body weight. You will need to make some effort to stand again on your own two feet otherwise family members and outsiders will be limited in how much they can help you. We each have that responsibility over ourselves and must be willing to admit that and do what is within our means. When we make that little effort, it means that the support others can give to us will be greater and much more effective. When we take no responsibility for our own healing and recovery and expect others to do it all for us, eventually they will not be able to hold our weight and will have to let go. Sometimes we may need a stronger hand to help us and at other times only a slight bit of support. That is alright, as long as throughout we are trying our best to make that effort to help our own selves.

Chapter 4

TRIALS AS OPPORTUNITIES

As with all things in life, particularly the trials of life, the very first thing we need to do if we are to utilise it as an opportunity to develop ourselves and grow wiser, stronger and closer to Allah ﷻ, is to do some introspection. That is not the same thing as blaming ourselves and drowning in that self blame. In the case of domestic abuse, the perpetrator will have usually done enough of blaming the victim and the object is not to continue the abuse.

The purpose of this introspection is like a safety net in order to ensure that we are being sincere and striving to be our best, for the sake of Allah ﷻ. This introspection is about checking our own deeds and actions and admitting places where we may have been at fault to Allah ﷻ alone and making firm intentions to intend to stay away from repeating those mistakes. There may be places where we need to rectify certain actions or there may not. There may be people we need to speak to, in order to explain why we may have behaved in an odd or unusual manner. There is always forgiveness for the one who asks and is sincere. This does not mean that we should be going and trying to pour our deepest self reflections to the perpetrator; it is not about the perpetrator at all. Rather it is about us and fixing our relationship with ourselves and other people, for that ultimately is a reflection of our relationship with Allah ﷻ. Often times it sadly will not be possible to have such a reasonable conversation with the perpetrator themselves hence why that is not being recommended here.

Those who have experienced domestic abuse also need to accept that there may have been occasions where you lost control and gave in to the utter confusion and chaos that was going on in your mind by lashing out at the perpetrator, but that this was not something you would have done in normal circumstances. It is possible that a perpetrator psychologically causes so much harm to an individual that the only way to vent their frustration that is simply beyond description is by almost losing control, if not actually losing control. You need to understand that you have been pushed to this and it was not after one or two 'mild' incidents so to speak, for in reality abuse is abuse. You therefore do not have to beat yourself up about such occasions as the perpetrator would want, but understand it in the context that it took place and all that led up to it and know that Allah ﷻ was your witness to all of this and more. In your introspection you want to move forward and build upon your experience, not self destruct. You do not need to do that, you have that choice. There will be strong days and more challenging days, but eventually it will get easier.

This leads onto the next point of understanding, realising and accepting that you have the greatest help possible, a source of help that were the whole world to gather to try and provide for you, they would be unable to do so. This is the help of Allah ﷻ, for He has promised and taken an Oath on His Honour that He will help the oppressed though it may be after a while.

The Prophet ﷺ said, **"There are three types of people whose invocations are not rejected; the just leader, the fasting person, and a wronged person. Allah would raise the latter's invocation over the clouds, where the gates of heaven are opened up for it and say, 'By My Honour, I shall support you, though after a while.'"**[14]

---

14 Jami' at-Tirmidhi, hadith number 2526

Allah ﷻ does not lie and nor does He make mention of an Oath lightly. Knowing this alone should be enough for us all to understand the special and unique position you hold with Allah ﷻ and should send chilling fears down the spine of every perpetrator. Who would dare to challenge Allah ﷻ? A perpetrator does just that by continuing the abuse and not rectifying their actions. The reality therefore is that you have nothing to worry about. Your Protector is Allah ﷻ Himself, and even if it seems the perpetrator is getting away with their crimes, they cannot escape Allah ﷻ. At some point in time they will face the consequences of their actions and should it be whilst they have not sought your forgiveness, repented and rectified their wrongdoings, then Allah ﷻ is the Most Just and does not wrong anyone by even an atom's weight. When a person truly ponders upon this, you will realise that you can actually pity the perpetrator for all that they have on their account of deeds. You, on the other hand, were the one that was wronged and therefore only served to elevate your status with Allah ﷻ insha'Allah, but now need to continue that growth in more healthy ways.

Chapter 5

DEALING WITH ANGER AND RESENTMENT

For some victims of domestic abuse, some of the degrading things that they have been subject to will naturally lead onto feeling a lot of anger and resentment for all that they were put through. A person would not be human if they did not feel some anger and resentment. You do however have a choice in how you deal with that anger and where you channel such emotions.

You can choose to focus on it and not move beyond it. This will quickly eat you up and destroy you from the inside out. It will fester away within you and gradually you will find that both your mental state and your physical health start to deteriorate to the point where functioning every day can be a challenge. The other thing you can do is to admit that you have anger within you and resent what you were put through, accept that you have a right to feel angry as your basic rights were taken away, but also accept that you do not necessarily have to act upon that anger and can release it in alternative healthy ways. In order to do that requires a lot of inner strength. A person who can hold themselves back from retaliating is an extraordinarily strong person and if you make your intention to be purely for the sake of Allah ﷻ, then you will have gained sustained strength that others cannot break.

You may feel that in your circumstances you need justice and indeed pursuing this through legal means is not wrong and cannot be faulted, especially if it is to restore rights to yourself and others and even to protect yourself and others in the future. You must however ensure that it is done through the proper legal means and that it is not just a form of you taking things to a level where you then end up being the perpetrator or re-enacting what they put you through to the same or a greater degree. That would then put you on the same level as the perpetrator and would not actually eradicate any of your feelings of anger or resentment. Remember that once you act upon that anger, it can easily overtake you as it runs through your veins and thus instead of being the oppressed, you would have now become the oppressor. Realise what the consequences of this can be in terms of both worldly life and what your goals in life are for the hereafter and whether it is worth taking the risk of things getting out of hand and you having the title of being an oppressor before Allah ﷻ.

There are numerous healthy ways in which you can release the tension of the anger which you feel. This may be talking it out through professional help with a therapist or other trained professional, taking up some sort of sporting activity that allows you to let out your frustration and tension, or writing down your feelings of anger and exploring why you feel this way, what would happen if you acted on the anger and how you can instead use it in a positive manner. When we understand the reasons behind our emotions, it then becomes easier for us to find the appropriate way to deal with it. For each person there will be something different but you do have that healthy alternative. You do not have to self destruct with those emotions.

Chapter 6

FORGIVENESS

When we forgive someone who has wronged us, we give ourselves permission to not be held back, to move forward, to free ourselves and taste the sweetness of not being chained to the past. Our hearts are set free to embrace the future. When we do not forgive, our hearts become consumed with this resentment that only builds up more and more and holds us back. Our chest constricts, our world darkens, and we only punish ourselves and cause ourselves misery which then spreads to those around us. Not forgiving does not harm the perpetrator but it does harm us.

The question that will naturally arise in anyone's mind is how can you forgive someone who has harmed you so much that they almost made you insane or almost killed you or the children, or paralysed you for life? Someone who was simply ruthless and utterly barbaric? The answer is that it is not humanly impossible but it is a high calling. Victims of domestic abuse have seen the worst of what humans can do to one another. For those who are fortunate enough to get help and support, they are then presented with the polar opposite by receiving the very best of what humans can offer to each other – that compassion, sincere care and support. It is something to ponder about. What lessons are there to learn from this? It shows the wide spectrum that humans can embrace and the results of that spectrum. We all have a choice in where we decide to be along that scale, every last one of us.

This forgiveness and going one step beyond by doing good, instead of harm in return, is the peak of excellence in patience that is mentioned by Allah ﷻ in the Qur'an. It is no easy feat as no peak ever is, but the challenge of achievement beckons every soul. That is the high calling. It means stamping out one's own ego and overcoming one's own anxieties and pain. It means doing it for a greater purpose. It means understanding our purpose in life and that this is in essence a direct way to gain such a status with Allah ﷻ Himself, that this can only be an opportunity.

> **"The good deed and the evil deed cannot be equal. Repel (the evil) with one which is better, then verily he, between whom and you there was enmity, (will become) as though he was a close friend. But none is granted it except those who are patient – and none is granted it except the owner of the great portion in this world."** [Qur'an 41:34-35]

True healing will only begin with forgiveness and leaving the past behind. The only person that loses out by not forgiving ends up being the victim themselves. It does not mean you have to be best friends with the perpetrator or even inform them of your forgiveness, especially if they have not asked for it or shown any repentance. It just means that you have understood that they have a lot to account for and you in reality can have the upper hand. But you are not like them and you choose not to be, hence neither would you actually wish for them to suffer, particularly in the hereafter.

Forgiveness does not mean that what they inflicted on you was right or correct in any way whatsoever – it is not about justifying their actions. Rather forgiveness is a reflection of what lies within your heart and a reflection of yourself. Rectifying their wrongdoing lies squarely with the perpetrator and for someone to forgive their perpetrator, they need not concern themselves with this if they choose not to. Being fixated on what the perpetrator has done will only waste valuable time and opportunity for you to move on with your life. Be sure to know that they will have to face Allah ﷻ and that there is no better justice than that. So once you know that, it does not prove fruitful to then waste the rest of your life thinking of all that has happened except to take valuable lessons forward for your own personal development and growth.

Forgiving means a lot of soul searching, understanding our purpose in life and the reality of life itself and the nature of humans. The reality is that we do not have the time to concentrate on the actions of others except to help put an end to oppression and ensure that in our own lives, we are living to the best human standards that we possibly can. When you remember that you were the wronged person and everything that your perpetrator put you through is now on his account of deeds, unless he repents and rectifies his wrongs, then you will realise that in reality you have the stronger position. Would you want to be in his shoes and have to answer for all that he has done? Thus, when the true meaning of this dawns upon you, you may find that you actually feel sympathy towards your perpetrator. They have a lot to answer for. You on the other hand have *du'as* that will be answered and a special status. You have your life back and can build yourself a positive future. You do not have the weight of all his wrongdoings to carry around with you wherever you may go. Yes he may not realise it right now, but one day it will hit him but that should not be your concern. You are not responsible for making your perpetrator understand the seriousness of their crimes and in a lot of cases you would be putting yourself at risk if you were to try. You now have your own purpose in life to concentrate upon.

Chapter 7

FINDING YOURSELF AGAIN

One of the biggest dilemmas that faces someone who has experienced domestic abuse is the sudden loss of identity. They have had this eradicated from all they have known, their personality has been squashed and stamped out, they may feel like a mere shadow of their former selves. They start to look to finding themselves again.

We are seeking the answers in the wrong place. The reality is that we need to be looking to find Allah ﷻ again. That is what we have lost. When your life is totally engrossed in the acts of the perpetrator and trying to survive their daily onslaught in whatever form it may be, the focus of your life becomes this survival and this perpetrator. But that is not our purpose in life. We haven't lost ourselves; we have lost that focus on our Creator and the purpose of our life.

This is where you need to start and from this you will find your feet and grounding again. This will give you that stability and the true foundation that we all need for our lives, for rebuilding, for growth and development. When you spend time contemplating and re-learning about our Creator and the message He has sent to us, life will once again begin to take its proper perspective and things will start to make sense again. You will begin to understand again why you are here and what you should be focussing on. It will require you to be brutally honest with yourself in examining your lives and your self, what you do, how you do it and why. The integral part of this is ensuring that we are living in a way that is in accordance to how Allah ﷻ wanted us to live and this also includes ensuring that we maintain an upright character.

We know that the final Messenger ﷺ was a living and breathing example of the Qur'an, the very word of Allah ﷻ and these are the footsteps that we need to follow. You do not need to be self destructive by having unrealistic expectations of yourself or putting yourself down; that is not the purpose and will only lead to negativity, depression and regression. If you want to find yourself again, you need to be the servant of God that Allah ﷻ wanted you to be, understanding that you will never reach perfection but that you do not have to stop striving to be the very best that you can be. This should be what your daily life revolves around because you are now trying to live with that constant consciousness of Allah ﷻ in your every deed as opposed to the burdening consciousness of a dominating perpetrator.

So this identity that you may feel you have lost is in reality a call from the depths of your soul to return your focus back to your Maker and be who He wanted you to be. That is where you will find the peace that you are seeking. You may continue to make mistakes along the way, but this is part of the process of returning to your Lord, humbled with experience and understanding and insha'Allah, wisdom. This is what will make you stronger and help you build those stable solid foundations that then cannot be taken advantage of in the future. This is what will grant you that freedom and liberation to be the best human being that you possibly can be. This is where you can find yourself again.

Chapter 8

'LEARNING TO TRUST AGAIN

Trusting anyone ever again after having been through domestic abuse, may seem like an impossible task. The one person closest to you who you entrusted with your very self, has betrayed you and broken that trust and therefore naturally, all your guards will go up as a measure of self protection.

However, this one person does not represent the rest of the world and all the people in it. The world around you is still the same and people will still be the same, it is just that your perception of the world has now changed. We humans are all in the same boat, we all have human traits and characteristics. That means that sometimes we will let others down whether intentionally or inadvertently. It also means we have the capacity to help each other and support each other in our goals and aspirations and most importantly in our purpose of life. Some people will be suitable for help and support in some areas and not in others and vice versa.

So who do you trust? You can start by trusting yourself based upon having the right intentions behind all that you do. Before this however, what should be underlying your very being is the fact that essentially you are placing your trust in Allah ﷻ. We know that humans are humans and therefore may let us down at times, but we also know that when we do something for the sake of Allah ﷻ and in accordance to what is pleasing to Allah ﷻ, then we are trusting Him to take us to a good outcome whatever that may be. Sometimes that goodness may be surrounded by difficulties and hardships, other times it may be easier and happier occasions. The responsibility of learning the lessons behind life events lies with us, but we can trust that with the right intentions, we are placing our trust in Allah ﷻ ultimately and humans are just part of the chain that make the cogs go round.

Whatever we experience of life, there will always be some good in it, lessons to be derived, examples to be taken, reflections to be had and changes for the future. But if we do not seek out what these are then life will remain stagnant, with no learning, no new experiences and no self development. It has been said that the definition of insanity is doing the same thing over and over and yet expecting different results. If we close our minds to learning and acting upon what we have learnt, we cannot expect there to be any changes in outcomes.

On a more practical level in terms of trust, it may be that you need to review your boundaries with people, yourself and different situations in order to protect you from those who will let you down and break your trust in a harmful way. You do not necessarily have to expose yourself to those whom you know will not be able to fulfil their trusts and that forms part of having healthy boundaries. You can choose who you reveal what to and in what depth. You do not need to tell the whole world everything about yourself and therefore leave yourself open to vulnerability. We all do this naturally on a daily basis, but when a person has had their trust broken they can lock down and take the stance of not trusting anyone at all because of previous negative experiences and violations of trust. This is also something that you do not need to do because by doing that you only end up isolating yourself when in actual fact there are trustworthy people out there who would be able to support you and help you get to where you wish to be if you allow them in and give them some trust. On the other hand, you may need time to understand what it means to have boundaries and not be too open with everyone that you meet, thus making them feel uncomfortable and leaving you open to being taken advantage of.

Coming out of an abusive relationship will have shifted all of your boundaries so that you may not fully understand healthy boundaries, hence it is important that you take care whom you allow into your life and to what extent. There will be people very close to you who you can confide in and who will keep that trust and give you the support you need. There will then be others who you hold at a slight distance, so you may reveal some personal things to them but not as much as those who are very close to you. Then there are those who you would only interact with as much as is required and would not reveal personal issues to them. It may be that this is not the appropriate context or because these individuals will not be able to receive and hold the information you convey and thus end up harming you whether intentionally or not. With others still, you will maintain further distance as they may be someone you only know in one certain capacity and once again, it is not appropriate to reveal personal information to them. None of these individuals in any of these scenarios have a right to know anything confidential about you except if you are happy to share it with them out of your own willingness.

One of the challenging aspects of setting boundaries that you may find is realising that some of those people who you thought were very close to you and that you could trust and talk to on a personal level previously, you actually cannot discuss what you have been through with them for various reasons. It may be because they simply are not able to understand what you have been through and thus may end up harming you when they mean well, or it may be that they do not know how to support you. It may be because they prove to be judgmental towards you and again this will stem from a lack of understanding of what you have been through and the impact it has had on you. Or it may just be that they do not want to know the personal details of your life. You do not need to let any of this drag you down and these do not have to become your issues. Their baggage does not need to become yours. You need positive individuals around you who will give you that healthy understanding and support and therefore if you are met with those who cannot provide you with that, you will be able to find that support elsewhere, it might just take some searching in cases where there is still a lot of isolation.

Of course when it is close family members and friends who you really thought you could rely on, it will naturally cause some grief and anguish. However accepting that humans are humans, regardless of being family or not, will help you to realise that by keeping a safe distance it will only protect you from further harm. For those who have missed out on that opportunity to help a fellow human in need, if not a blood relative, that is the reality for them; they have missed out on an opportunity to do good.

Ultimately this is the greatest opportunity for us to learn to rely on Allah ﷻ and perhaps His way of teaching us this valuable lesson. It of course helps to have people around us who can support us and give us a helping hand but their help will be limited to what is within both their capability and our capacity to act upon. It is in finding inner strength that we will truly have real strength in which to see through any of the challenges of life. That inner strength can only come from knowing that as long as we strive to please our Creator in all of our actions and deeds, then He will be there to give us the strength and support that we need to face whatever challenges may come along the paths that we tread. Turning to Allah ﷻ and asking of Him will essentially provide us with solid foundations that will then enhance the effectiveness of the help and support that others are able to give, because it will mean that we are more able to help ourselves through the Grace of Allah ﷻ and thus having further human support in addition to that will insha'Allah act as a final supplement. This will also make it easier for us to bear the pain of anyone who may let us down or who we realise cannot be included in that close circle around us. In every challenge we face there are valuable lessons to learn and act upon, we are not relying upon people, but they can potentially provide us with some support hence the importance of healthy boundaries and allowing that human help. We are relying upon Allah ﷻ and thus can rest assured that there is a good reason behind everything that happens.

Relying on Allah ﷻ also does not mean that you can just open up to anyone and everyone. Rather the opposite; we hold our reliance in Allah ﷻ as the grounding for all our other relationships but we make sure that we do our part of maintaining healthy distances where we need to, while allowing others in to support us where they can fulfil this. As with everything in life, you want that middle path for your best recovery and progression in life, not to veer off to extremes either way that will only be detrimental to your health, well being, recovery and hereafter. It is this that will then enable you to have rebuilt your life and live it in a more fulfilling way, both in accordance to what our Creator wants of us and to what you personally need.

FINAL WORDS

Domestic Violence is an epidemic that is not going away in the near future. Unless we stand up and make some noise about this oppression it will only continue to exacerbate, especially considering the growing Muslim population. If we want change for our future generations then we need to start planting the seeds now.

Domestic violence is a very sensitive area to deal with and oftentimes people can be unsure of how to help others, though they sincerely wish to. If you know of someone who is currently going through domestic abuse, or you have very strong indications that they are but are not sure what to do then the following is a very general guideline, bearing in mind the safety of that individual and any children:

1. Try to ascertain whether there is domestic violence going on if possible. Very often asking directly is the wrong way to go about this as it may worry the individual especially if she is in danger, and make her pull away from you further.

2. Reassure the individual in general terms that she has you to turn to and can come to you for anything, so that she knows she does have somewhere to turn to. Do not put any pressure on her to confide anything to you. She needs to be able to seek help at her own pace and in accordance to what she knows is the safest way and time.

3. If she does confide in you then try and get her in touch with professional help and advice with regards to the situation. If it is the case that she has to leave for her own safety and that of any children then professional, timely and sensitive help is all the more important.

4. Be there to support her as much as you can without applying any pressure and without passing any judgements upon her. Do not put any pressure on her to leave as this could increase the danger she is in.

5. The most dangerous time for a victim of domestic violence is when she is leaving/has just left. The risk from perpetrators is at its greatest at this point hence why professional help is crucial. You should not be afraid to call the relevant authorities for assistance if required.

6. If you know of someone who you overwhelmingly suspect is going through domestic violence but you have no way of communicating with them about it, for example, a neighbour that always avoids you yet you have clearly heard unhealthy patterns from their household, or you have witnessed anything out in public, you can always call the authorities anonymously if you do not wish to give your name and give your concerns / descriptions / names of individuals / addresses of concern / number plates of cars that you may have witnessed abuse occurring in etc.

7. If someone has left their husband and is in need of a lot of support, you do not have to deal with it all by yourself. Enlist the help of other trustworthy people and any professional services that you can. Always double check with the individual first though before you do anything on her behalf and make sure she is comfortable with it and does not find it a threat in any way.

We all need to do what we can as much as we are able, for at some point in our lives we sadly will come across someone who has been through this epidemic and may need our help.

For those women who are still going through such horrendous treatment or have been through it, know that there is a way out. I hope that this book will demonstrate that and show you that you can and do have a future ahead of you and for what you have gone through, you will be greatly recompensed.

To all perpetrators, my sincere advice is to change now before it is too late for you, for your own sake. In the long run you will be the greatest loser otherwise.

To my fellow community members, we all have different responsibilities, let us start living up to them even just on a basic human level. Change can happen if we all do our little bit.

BIBLIOGRAPHY

The Noble Qur'an

Men are from Mars, Women are from Venus: John Gray, Thorsons 2005

Oppression and the Oppressors: Mohamed Moutwalli Shaaraoui, Translated by Chafik Abdelghani, Al Firdous Ltd 2006

Riyad as-Salihin: Al-Imam Abu Zakariya Yahya bin Sharaf An-Nawawi, Translated by Mahomed Mahomedy, Zam Zam Publishers 2008

The Battered Woman: Lenore E Walker, Harper & Row 1979

The Emotionally Abusive Relationship: Beverly Engel, John Wiley & Sons 2002

The Verbally Abusive Relationship: Patricia Evans, Adams Media 2010

Trauma and Recovery: Judith Herman MD, Basic Books 1997

Why Does He Do That: Lundy Bancroft, Berkley Books 2002

Why Mars and Venus Collide: John Gray, Harper Element 2008

Websites

www.ons.gov.uk: Office for National Statistics

www.womensaid.org.uk: Womens Aid

www.youtube.com: What women need to know about men, Shaykh Yasir Qadhi, 2013. https://www.youtube.com/watch?v=Jf6B4xk3kcI

www.youtube.com: What men need to know about women, Shaykh Yasir Qadhi, 2013. https://www.youtube.com/watch?v=VR395_rb8pc&nohtml5=False

www.facebook.com: Mufti Menk, 2012. https://www.facebook.com/muftimenk/posts/10150662000486971

Journal Papers

Lees (2000), *The Effects of Rape and Domestic Violence on Health* in *British Psychological Society*, Women's Health: An International Reader, London: British Psychological Society

GLOSSARY OF ISLAMIC TERMS

﷾   *subhanahu wa ta'ala* means 'glorious and exalted is He' and is used after the term Allah [God]

ﷺ   *sallallahu alayhi wa sallam* means 'may the peace and blessings of Allah be upon him' and is said after every mention of the name of the Prophet Muhammad ﷺ

        radhiallahu anhu means 'may Allah be pleased with him' and is used after the name of the male Companions of the Prophet Muhammad ﷺ

        radhiallahu anha means 'may Allah be pleased with her' and is used after the names of the female members of the Prophet's household and his female Companions

Aishah   one of the wives of the Prophet Muhammad ﷺ

deen   religion; life transaction

insha'Allah   if Allah wills

Khadijah   the first wife of the Prophet Muhammad ﷺ

nikah   the legal contract of marriage in Islam

qawwamoon   this is the term used in the Qur'an (4:34) to describe the role of men. It has been translated in various ways by translators of the Qur'an: 'protectors and maintainers' (Yusuf Ali); 'take full care of' (Asad); 'in charge of' (Pickthall). It comes from the root word meaning 'to stand' or 'to establish'.

sabr   patience, forbearance in the face of difficult circumstances